BAD LADS

BAD LADS

RAF National Service Remembered

Alf Townsend

SUTTON PUBLISHING

This book is dedicated to Nicolette, my lovely wife of almost fifty years. Without her continuing love and support through the terrible days when we lost our eldest daughter Jenny to breast cancer, I wouldn't have been able to survive – let alone write three books.

We've had some tragic times during our long marriage, as well as many wonderful years with our three lovely children and, now, our seven grandchildren. They say a man is nothing without a good woman and I know I am lucky enough to have a truly great lady!

First published in 2006 by
Sutton Publishing Limited · Phoenix Mill
Thrupp · Stroud · Gloucestershire · GL5 2BU

British Library Cataloguing in Publication Data
A catalogue record for this book is available from the British Library.

ISBN 0-7509-4154-5

Title-page picture: On parade. *(RAF Museum, Hendon)*

Typeset in 11/15pt Sabon.
Typesetting and origination by
Sutton Publishing Limited.
Printed and bound in England by
J.H. Haynes & Co. Ltd, Sparkford.

CONTENTS

FOREWORD

Alf Townsend has been associated with the London taxi-trade press for as long as I can remember. He was a founder member of the LTDA (Licensed Taxi-Driver's Association) more than three decades ago and started writing articles for its publication, *Taxi*, in the early 1970s. Some years – and many hundreds of articles later – he was invited to join the newly launched *Taxi Globe* as a feature writer. He moved on to *London Taxi Times* some years later, then finally the *Cab Driver Newspaper*.

Alf always writes what he thinks is the truth, and over the years his hard-hitting and down-to-earth comments have often upset many notables in the trade. But many of his regular readers enjoy his fortnightly humorous columns in which he is forever poking fun at the establishment. He has always involved himself in the trade that he loves. For many years he played for Mocatra (motor-cab trade) football team, and later joined the newly formed Golf Society. He has also organised cab-trade golf tournaments, cadging sponsorship from major companies and taking the qualifiers to Spain for a free holiday.

In the early 1990s, Alf was appointed as the senior LTDA trade representative at Heathrow Airport. He helped to form the cab-driver's co-operative HALT (Heathrow Airport Licensed Taxis) and eventually became its chairman. Alf then started the HALT magazine and, almost unaided, produced and edited it for the first five years or more. The HALT magazine became a popular twenty-page, full-colour front and back publication, which was popular among the cabbies at Heathrow and always showed a small profit.

In the late 1990s, after tragically losing his eldest daughter Jenny to breast cancer, Alf decided to give up all his political positions to concentrate on writing books. *Bad Lads* is his second book and Alf is hoping that it proves as popular as his first book *Cabbie*.

Dave Allen
Editor, *Cab Driver Newspaper*

INTRODUCTION

Sadly, these are violent times. Street crime is escalating, as are teenage crime and drug abuse. Parents are struggling to keep their kids in check, with little success. It seems as though many young people, not only from the deprived, inner-city areas but also from middle-class suburban families, are totally out of control. At the present time even the police are finding it very difficult to prosecute minors and some of the very worst tearaways, guilty of dozens of petty crimes, are still walking away from our courts having been ordered to pay minimal fines or waste time, in my humble opinion, in useless community service. What must be particularly galling to the police is the attitude of the small, vociferous group of 'liberals' who believe passionately that these kids are not responsible for their actions; consequently, the punishments meted out hardly ever match the crimes.

Some experts put this breakdown in family living down to the fact that in some cases both parents are forced to work to support their household, while others consider drugs are the cause. Whatever your age, if you are hooked you'll do just about anything for a 'fix'. It seems that unless there is a change in the law in the very near future, or a different attitude to teenage crime is adopted by the courts, kids will continue to run riot and cock a snook at civilised society without any fear of going to prison.

However, many parents have had enough and in the course of my job as an experienced London cabbie – hopefully you've read my first book *Cabbie* – I've started hearing more mature passengers harking back to the halcyon days of national service in the 1950s. Older dads are particularly forthright in airing their views, stating categorically that bringing back national service could well solve the escalating problem of teenage crime almost overnight! After more than four decades of driving a taxi, I'm a good listener and, like many other experienced cabbies, I'm adept at tuning in to the feelings of the general public and even the present state of the economy. Did you know that many City high-flyers gauge the economic situation by the number of taxis purchased every quarter? They reckon that if the cabbies are busy and buying new taxis, then the economy must be buoyant and a recession is not on the horizon!

But I digress. This latest interest shown in national service has been highlighted by various reality television shows on the subject. So I thought that it was now the appropriate time to write a book describing the highs and lows of my time as a lowly aircraftman second class in the RAF in the early 1950s. Before national service I'd been heading down the criminal road at top speed. It was about par for the course to do a bit of thieving if you were raised in North London, or anywhere else in London come to that!

The downhill spiral started with petty thieving in 'Woolies' in Chapel Market, descended to breaking into deserted and often bombed-out factories and nicking the plate glass to flog to the local shop who made fish-tanks, then lifting the 'bluey' (the lead) from roofs and making a nice few quid from the local scrapyard. Moving quickly up the crime ladder, I became a part-time 'doggie', a look-out, for an illegal street bookmaker, mixing with hardened criminals who had done time on 'The Moor' (Dartmoor) and in 'The Ville' (Pentonville Prison). These hard men, with their stories of 'blagging' and 'shooters', made a big impression on a youngster like me. I liked their flash, expensive suits and the way they pulled a wad of 'readies' out of their pockets to have a bet on the gee-gees. I listened to them talking about the guv'nors of the London crime scene. They spoke in reverent tones about Billy Hill, Jack Spot, Albert Dimes and the Maltese gangs that ran the Mayfair brothels. Yet even these tough and brutal gang-leaders had eventually to make way for a bunch of cold-eyed killers from South London. Nobody, but nobody, messed with the Richardson gang, with big Freddie Foreman and 'Mad' Frankie Fraser. If you did, then you could well find yourself in a concrete coffin in the English Channel or part of the foundations of the new M4 motorway!

Slowly but surely I began to model myself on these local villains. I got nicked a few times for petty thieving and was sent away for a 'holiday'. The villains just laughed, especially when I returned. 'That's nuffink kiddo; wait until you do some hard-time', they used to say jokingly. But there were a couple of major things that prevented me from going further down the criminal road. First was my passion for football and the fact that I had been invited to join a professional club as an apprentice pro. However, with the benefit of hindsight, doing my national service in the RAF really made a man out of me. I went in reluctantly as a mere slip of a boy, concerned only about myself and what was in it for me, and always on the look-out for an illegal 'fiddle'. Yet, in a matter of about only six weeks this yobbo from up the 'Cally' (Caledonian Road) had been moulded into a conscientious humanbeing who pulled his full weight for the rest of his hut. Far be it for me to say that reintroducing national service would cure all of the problems among today's teenagers in one fell swoop. But I know, in my heart of hearts, that without national service I would now be doing 'hard-time' in a Category A nick like many of my old mates – some of whom spent half of their lives behind bars.

This is my story of RAF national service in the 1950s and maybe the catalyst for some of the other 3 million or so young men who were made to do their time. After a period of half a century or more, some of the facts have dimmed in my mind. That's when I have resorted to artistic licence and embellishment in an effort to keep the story interesting. The places and the characters are real and only the names have been changed to avoid any embarrassment – or any possible libel charges or a thick ear! Many people, including me, thoroughly enjoyed Leslie Thomas's great book of the 1960s, *The Virgin Soldiers* – I suppose this is a bit like *The Virgin Airmen*!

ROYAL AIR FORCE

SWIMMING PROFICIENCY CERTIFICATE

This is to certify that 2592442 Aircraftman Townsend

on 1st June 1953, *at* Walsall Baths

attained the following standards in swimming:—

Swam 150 *yards continuously using the following strokes for* 50 *yards each:—*

i. *Breast stroke.*

ii. *Back stroke and*

iii. *Free style (other than* (i.) *or* (ii.)).

[illegible] Sqn Ldr for *Officer Commanding* Royal Air Force Hednesford.

RAF swimming certificate awarded to the author in 1953. *(Author's collection)*

CHAPTER ONE

BEFORE THE RAF

The year was 1952. The old King had just passed away and his eldest daughter Elizabeth had been hastily recalled from her tour of Kenya to take up the mantle of sovereign of the United Kingdom and what remained of the old British Empire.

I had been back in London for some seven years since the end of the Second World War, following my bitter and sometimes brutal stay in Cornwall as an evacuee in the care of some wicked people purely in it for the money. Strangely enough, despite my traumatic experiences and apart from ongoing and horrific nightmares, I had grown up a happy and quite intelligent teenager, always looking for a good laugh. I had sailed through the old 'eleven plus' exam and moved on to grammar school. I was a pretty good footballer, big, strong and raw-boned with decent heading ability and a fierce shot in either foot. I soon became captain of the school team when I was selected to play for Islington Schoolboys and South of England Schoolboys.

I recall one match in particular against Edmonton Schoolboys. Their captain and star was a tiny little chap called Johnny Haynes, who, as most people remember, eventually became captain of Fulham and England. He was the very first footballer to be paid a massive £100 a week in wages! Their other star was their left-winger Trevor Chamberlain, known to all the boys as 'Tosh'. Now, Tosh was one of those very early developers; in fact, he was a man in *all* parts while we were still boys. He had massive shoulders, a deep-barrelled, hairy chest and his legs were like solid tree trunks. And couldn't he whack a football with his trusty left peg? Tosh must have been the hardest dead-ball kicker of his era. He rose through the international ranks of schoolboy football with Johnny Haynes, and like Johnny he played for Fulham for many seasons. Yet, he never possessed

Johnny's natural skills, and the classier defenders soon tumbled that Tosh was only one-footed. So they forced him out to the touchline and he could hardly ever exploit his explosive shooting with that famous left peg. Nevertheless, Tosh was one of the best young footballers I've ever seen. Incidentally, as I recall, we lost 8–0 to Edmonton Schoolboys on that fateful day – and I believe the 'little fella' scored a hat trick!

It seems strange that with a background of being dragged up in a North London slum, and apparently only happy when I was kicking a ball around, I had a love of anything remotely to do with writing, which was nurtured by my lovely old English teacher. He was forever telling me that I had a talent for writing and that I needed to move on to university to improve my literary knowledge. But these were very hard times in post-war London. My old Mum was struggling to feed her growing youngsters, hindered by a work-shy husband who was at his happiest when visiting most of the pubs up the Caledonian Road. As the eldest son, my wages were desperately needed to help the family budget. So I left school before the final exams, just to help to put food on the table for our family. I certainly wasn't unique in this situation: many of my school friends at the time were far more talented than me, but likewise their poverty stricken parents urgently required them to help keep the family in food. I must confess that I often imagine what might have been if only I had gone on to university. But for the most part I've been more than happy and contented with my life, with my lovely wife, my kids and now my grandchildren.

So, I had left school and now I badly needed a job. My old Mum's three surviving brothers, since one had been killed in the Desert Campaign against Rommel in the Second World War, all worked down the old Covent Garden Market as porters. I bashed their ears every time I visited them, and they eventually found me a job in the market. It wasn't much, but it was paid work nonetheless, and I took home a few quid every week – plus my daily bag of fruit and veg. This item was known to all the market workers as a 'cochell', but where the name comes from I do not know. It was one of those customs that probably dates back to the Victorian era, and even the 'Beadles', the market police, didn't dare stop one of the market workers with his cochell. They had probably been forewarned by the bosses, who knew they'd have a strike on their hands if they attempted to stop this ageless perk! Sadly, the old Covent Garden Market, full of colourful characters and customs, was moved to a sterile and clinical, custom-built site at Nine Elms in the late 1970s. The 'new' Covent Garden is now a pedestrianised area, a Mecca for tourists with its many boutiques, posh wine bars and restaurants.

By this time I was playing soccer for three different teams every weekend, plus the market team mid-week, with most of the players being years older than me. Then, out of the blue, there came a positive move forward in my blossoming football career. A scout had seen me playing over at Hackney Marshes and informed the guy who ran Leyton Orient Juniors that he wanted me to come down for a trial in Chertsey, Surrey. I was most impressed with the greeting I received when I exited the station. The man in charge met me in an old vintage 'Roller' and took me for lunch to a very posh gaff. His name was Mr Loftus-Tottenham, known to all the players as 'Tott', and he owned the firm 'Chase of Chertsey', which made greenhouses, cloches and the like, and was the official name for the Leyton Orient Juniors at that time. Tott was quite old; well, he looked old to me. He was very tall, had grey hair and horn-rimmed specs and was well dressed. He spoke with an impeccable public-school accent. However, in essence he was an out and out football nut, who spent bundles of his own money in supplying Leyton Orient FC with promising young apprentice footballers.

I soon learned that Tott's one burning ambition was to discover a future English international star. I recall that his star protégé at the time of my arrival on the scene was a guy called Derek Healey. Now, this guy was red hot and could do almost anything with a football during our training sessions. He would head the ball forever, then he'd juggle it on either knee and cushion it on his neck for a very spectacular finale. Tott was convinced that he'd finally found his future England international. Sadly, Derek didn't make it as a professional. Like many talented ball players before him, he had the shit kicked out of him by the wily old-timers and quickly disappeared into obscurity. In fact, out of all the talented squad in the Chase of Chertsey team at that time, only one made the grade in the professional ranks. That was our centre-half Sid Bishop, who went on to play fourteen seasons in the Leyton Orient first team before retiring as a pub landlord. The jump from amateur to professional soccer is really tough and many talented youngsters never make it.

I played centre-forward for Chase of Chertsey for a couple of seasons. We won the league; I scored a lot of goals and got selected for the Surrey

Eleven. One day we played another county on the Orient ground at Brisbane Road. We won 4–1; I scored all four goals. After that triumph, my old Dad got a letter from Leyton Orient asking if I would like to join their ground staff as an apprentice professional. I couldn't wait to mix with the top pros and so I met the manager the following day and signed on the dotted line. All the while I played for Chase of Chertsey, Tott would pull me to one side and tell me that if I worked hard, I could become England's centre-forward one day in the future. I suppose dear old Tott is long gone now, but he was a lovely man and he gave me a big boost in my otherwise drab, miserable life. My only regret is that I never fulfilled his dream of my becoming an England international. Maybe it was the interruption of my career by national service, maybe it was a lack of effort on my part. Most probably it was because I never really had the God-given talent of someone like the inimitable Johnny Haynes. True, I could score plenty of goals against amateur players. But when I was matched against seasoned pros, they really gave me a lesson in dirty tricks and gamesmanship. I was just a boy playing for fun, coming up against grown men who played serious football for a living to feed and clothe their kids!

Sadly, I never made it to the top of the football ladder. I finished up earning a few quid a game as a part-time pro in the Southern League. Nevertheless, I thoroughly enjoyed my time on the ground staff at Leyton Orient and the buzz of finally being selected for their reserve team was electric. The fact that my début was against Millwall and that I was kicked from one end of the field to the other didn't seem to matter. I thought I was on my way to the top, so a few bruises were nothing! In retrospect, I'm happy that I was given the opportunity by the then manager of Leyton Orient, dear old Alec Stock, a lovely man. I mixed with guys who were household names at the time and was given my prized possession, my players' pass, which allowed me to sit on the touchline at any ground and at any league game. I could even stroll into the mighty Arsenal's ground and watch the top stars in action! I relished my short career as a minor celeb, as did my old Dad. He got many a free pint out of it whenever I got a write-up in the sports pages! His favourite ploy was to gather a bundle of the relevant newspapers and make a visit to most of the pubs up the Caledonian Road. His spiel was always the same: 'Did you read this in the paper about my son?', he would enquire of one of the guys at the bar. This invariably led to a free drink, or two or three! Nobody can ever take those memories away from me. So why am I prattling on about my early football ability, you may well be asking? Well, later on during my RAF national service this ability became the catalyst for many different happenings and so forms an integral part of my story.

Looking for a Way Out

Most of our Caledonian Road gang were about the same age, and all of us knew that national service was just around the corner. We used to sit for hours on street corners nervously talking about how we could wriggle out of it. Digressing slightly, I recall one day when we were all sitting on a wall at the top of our street and I noticed a group of girls gathering near a block of flats opposite. Being dead nosy and hoping to chat them up, we crossed the road to join them. It turned out that they were all members of the Johnny Ray Fan Club. Now, in the early 1950s, Johnny Ray, an American pop-singer, was the biggest thing to hit the UK since sliced bread! He was a skinny little bloke with a huge hearing-aid, and I thought his singing was crap. Nevertheless, his records sold in their thousands and he had been invited to come over and sing at the famous London Palladium. The girls told us with bated breath that the famous Johnny Ray was in the block of flats visiting the secretary of his fan club. So they all started screaming, 'John-nee, John-nee!', until eventually this little guy appeared on a balcony some six storeys up and started waving and singing his hit single 'Cry'. All the girls started swooning, while we shouted, 'You're crap, you can't sing to save your life!' Lovely, lovely memories, especially since dear old Johnny Ray died fairly recently. He really was the very first of the pop idols. Sadly, he finished his distinguished career by singing for peanuts in the bar of a Las Vegas casino.

For sure, we all had plenty of front and cockney chat, but when it came to giving up your life for Queen and Country, then it was a different ball game! The Korean War was looming on the horizon, and the distinct possibility of becoming cannon fodder in some foreign field made us extremely apprehensive. That prospect persuaded me from day one that the Army would never ever get me! We discovered various options that could be used as possible ways out. First was the use of deferments. These were only given to those going on to university or in apprenticeships, or those in important jobs like coal-mining. But even if we all moved up north and took up coal-mining, you still had to do your time when the job or the course had finished. So deferments weren't an option for our gang. The Merchant Navy didn't seem a bad choice. But, again, you had to serve the same time as national service, and, who knows, one day your ship might be bound for Korea with a full load of explosives and become a prime target for North Korean fighter planes – or even one of their submarines. Anyway, for somebody like me who could quite easily get seasick on the boating lakes at Finsbury Park or Hyde Park, the Merchant Navy definitely wasn't a viable alternative! That left going on the run, so the authorities couldn't trace you, or deliberately injuring yourself so that you would fail the medical. Many of my mates did go on the run when the time came, but they all got rounded up eventually and were still doing time in the 'Glasshouse' (the Army prison) long after I had finished my national service.

The only two guys I know of who beat the system were the notorious Kray twins. The Army couldn't break them despite their many months in a bad-boys' glasshouse, so they finally 'surrendered' and begrudgingly, gave both twins a 'DD', a Dishonourable Discharge. And as for deliberately injuring oneself to escape national service, as a fit young sportsman that never appealed to me. But I remember it was of interest to one of our gang. His name was Harry, and for obvious reasons his nickname was 'Crazy' Harry. There's always one nutter in any gang, isn't there? 'Crazy' Harry stated from day one that no way was he ever going to do national service, and he kept his promise. The guys told me that 'Crazy' Harry had stuck a pointed object deep into one of his ears and deliberately pierced his eardrum. Okay, so he beat the system. But, unfortunately, he suffered great pain for the rest of his life with mastoiditis and tragically died at an early age.

So, the rest of the gang had fully discussed the options in an effort to beat the system, but to no avail. It seemed inevitable that I, as a super-fit young athlete, would be forced to serve my Queen and Country, whether I liked it or not. I needed to sit down and carefully think about my possible courses of action. The Army was definitely out for me, even though many of my mates up the Cally eventually finished up in the Green Jackets and spent most of their time in Germany. And the only way you could get into the Royal Navy was to sign on for a minimum of nine years. So that was a no-no. That left the RAF, known to all my mates as the 'Brylcream Boys'. I had heard some gossip from the older lads who had done their time in the Army. They reckoned that whenever they were on manoeuvres in Germany and had to sleep under canvas the RAF detachment lived like lords in the local farmhouses with plenty of food, wine and home comforts. That sounded just my cup of tea, and I stored that rumour in my brain right up to the time of the selection board! I accepted the inevitable and soon before my eighteenth birthday the postman delivered another present, my call-up papers. I had to fill in the details on the form. 'I would like to join the RAF', I wrote, adding that I had a grammar-school education. Occupation? What the hell – I put down 'professional footballer', which was rather presumptuous to say the least. But it worked. I received another notice a few weeks later to report to the chief medical officer, I think it was in Theobalds Road, Holborn, and I knew that this was the RAF Medical Officer.

'Well then, airman, who's your four-legged friend?' *(RAF Museum, Hendon)*

I sailed through the medical as A1, a perfect young and healthy specimen of manhood. Even being asked to drop my trousers and 'bend over and cough' didn't bother me one little bit! The postman called again a couple of weeks later, and the letter gave me the news I was hoping for. My carefully laid plans had worked. I had managed to bypass the rigours and hardships of the Army and had been accepted into the RAF. Nobody, but nobody, wanted to do national service. But if it was inevitable, then it made sense to try and get into the service that was probably the cushiest number available.

A Travel Warrant to Padgate

For starters, I didn't have a clue as to the whereabouts of my destination of Padgate. But I knew it was somewhere up north, because my travel warrant instructed me to get the train from King's Cross on a given date and time.

The train was packed to the roof with young guys like me from all over the south of England, all in the same situation as me and all a wee bit nervous thinking what the future might hold for them. Many of the lads were from the suburbs and were quite posh, unlike myself, who had endured the stress and hardships of being an evacuee in the Second World War, without the support of my parents. For the most part, these posh lads had spent the war with their mums and dads in the relative safety of their comfortable suburban semis. Most of the posh blokes I got to talk to were okay, but one of them, a plonker called Nigel from Banstead near Croydon, was a pain in the arse. He was a tall, gangly youth, with long, unkempt hair, who was always prattling on about electronics and how he wanted to get into radar in the 'Raff'. It seemed he was the leader of the suburban pack, and his mates all called him 'Nige'. He was forever using the dopey expression of 'soopah-doopah' and saying 'yah' to everything in reply. Sod's Law being what it is, out of all the guys on the train I was lumbered with this pillock right through basic training. Even that wasn't the end of it. I had the misfortune to meet up with him later on after my punishment posting for allegedly assaulting an NCO and, would you 'Adam-and-Eve' it, he had made corporal!

However, as is often the case in adversity, the tribal instinct helped us all to bond together. Suddenly it didn't seem to matter that most of these suburban lads spoke with a funny posh accent. We were all in the same boat, even though many of my new-found friends on the train might well turn out to be POMs, potential officer material, in the future! But certainly not me – no way, Josay! All I wanted was a cushy posting near London where I could creep away every weekend to play my football. I planned to do my time without any aggro, but life's not like that one little bit, is it? Unfortunately, aggro follows you whether you want it or not – and I seemed to be the type that it followed!

Padgate, the Reception Camp

The officers and drivers in their RAF blue coaches waiting at the station had done it all a million times before. To them, we were simply another

A mixed bunch all right. The long and the short and the tall, from every walk of life. *(RAF Museum, Hendon)*

The author fifty-three years ago, ready to fight for Queen and Country. *(Author's collection)*

intake of nervous teenagers wondering what might lie ahead; and the sooner they got us to the camp, the sooner they could get into the NAAFI for a bevvy.

Lots of NCOs were wandering about with clipboards, all shouting out lots of different names, until eventually the coaches were loaded. It reminded me very much of 1941 and my waiting, absolutely terrified, with my gas mask and my brown identity label amid the hustle and bustle of Paddington station. As a 5-year-old kid, expecting to be going down to the 'seaside' for a day, I was in for a big shock as an evacuee. My 'day out' became almost five years away, with plenty of heartache!

The rest of the week at Padgate is a bit of a blur in my mind. We were allocated our billets, all the staff were chatty and very friendly, and it was almost like home from home. With the benefit of hindsight, I now realise that the staff at Padgate had a very easy number and none of them wanted to blot their copybook and get posted elsewhere! They kitted us out with those horrible, itchy, blue uniforms and huge boots that were large enough for us to walk on water! Then, another medical. 'Drop your trousers, bend over and cough', and, 'Have you ever had a rash or sores around your private parts?' Then, the nasty bit. Queuing up stripped to the waist and waiting for your 'jabs'. As I got closer and closer to the guy with the needle, I became increasingly queasy. My older mates had told me that many of the young conscripts would often faint with fright at the thought of the needle. Please, God, I thought, don't let it be me who's the wally. As luck happened – for me, anyway – the young guy in front of me fainted, and being an old Boy Scout I managed to grab him to stop him falling over and bashing his head. I then placed him in the recovery position, with my jacket under his head as a pillow. This act of impulsive 'gallantry' had the effect of clearing my head, and, bingo, my queasiness vanished. I even got a smile and a knowing look from the old doc, who looked absolutely bored out of his mind.

Next, it was the dreaded 'haircut'. I liked to think that I was a bit of a snappy dresser, and my hairstyle reflected this – nice and long down the sides, with a popular 'DA' at the back. It took me years to realise that DA stood for 'Duck's Arse'! I sat down in the chair and jokingly told the young airman who was wielding the scissors to take a bit off there and a little bit off here and to make sure he feathered my hair. He puffed away on his fag, then grunted in an indifferent fashion, having heard the same crap a

The author with his 'partner in crime'. Note the white stones outside that had to be painted with a toothbrush and the grass that was cut with small scissors if you were a naughty boy! *(Author's collection)*

million times before. Then, in a crazed orgy of sweet revenge, he proceeded to run amok with his electric clippers and almost shaved my oily locks to the bone! He sniffed loudly, probably with delight, and proceeded to shout out with a smirk on his face, 'And the next gentleman please to the scaffold!'

So, I was now the proud keeper of two sets of 'blues', one for work and one for best. One beret and one peaked hat that made me look like a postman. RAF issue shirts, ties, long-sleeved pullovers, underwear, socks and boots. A greatcoat, kitbag and backpack side packs and webbing-belts. Plus the indispensable 'mug and irons' for your grub. And I now had a service number: 2592442. Aircraftman Second Class, Townsend A.E. Not forgetting my important pay book, my 'twelve fifty' (1250). The weekly pay for an AC2 in those days was less than thirty bob a week. But hey, the front-line soldiers weren't getting much more and they were risking their lives. I certainly looked the part in my brand-new blues, and I thought the ladies back home might take a shine to this young airman with the shaven nut!

However, the Padgate 'party' was coming to an end. Everyone knew only too well that we had to endure some six weeks of recruit training – or 'square-bashing', as it was commonly known – in the very near future. Now, according to the RAF manual, new recruits were usually sent to the nearest training camp to their home. But 'usually' was an operative word that could be construed in any manner depending on the whims of the officers in charge. The 'choices' at the time were Bridgnorth, which was somewhere up north; Cardington, which I believe was somewhere in Wiltshire; and Hednesford, somewhere near Wolverhampton. So I plumped for the one in Wiltshire, which was nearest to London and my home. And hey presto, when they called me into the office and gave me the destination of my training camp, surprise surprise, it was Hednesford! Understanding the workings of the RAF later in my service, and their undoubted ability to put round pegs into square holes, I suppose I was lucky not to get posted to the farthest camp at Bridgenorth! Luckily, as it turned out this posting to Hednesford did me a few favours further down the line. I had been desperately looking for a posting near London to help further my football career, and being sent to do my square bashing at Hednesford eventually afforded me that golden opportunity!

So, one fine day we were instructed to pack up all our gear and head for the parade ground. Again, it was absolute bedlam, with lots of shouting and screaming from the NCOs as they tried to sort out names and numbers to load onto the blue RAF coaches all lined up waiting for us. Finally, we were up and away. What our camp was like and even where it was situated, nobody had a clue. But, deep down, most of us had the feeling of foreboding. Even I realised that the RAF just couldn't be as cushy as Padgate. The lads attempted to get a sing-song going on our coach, just as if we were off on a boozy pub outing. But I was in no mood to sing. None of these young suburban lads was streetwise, whereas I had a gut feeling that we were heading deep for 'Shit Street' and that feeling persisted for the whole journey!

CHAPTER TWO

SQUARE-BASHING AT RAF HEDNESFORD

The dozen or so coaches pulled into the camp at Hednesford and we all got up to leave. This was our first mistake, and one that the drill corporals were banking on. 'Get back onto the coaches you 'orrible lot!' screamed a frenzied voice. 'You only move when we tell you to bloody move. You're a bloody shambles, the lot of you, but I'm gonna change all that.' Yeah, the Padgate party really was over and this was serious stuff, I thought to myself.

There was the sound of heavy boots and heavy breathing climbing the steps of the coach, while we all beat a hasty retreat to our seats and sat there nervously. Then, our drill corporal appeared. He wore a smartly pressed uniform and glistening boots. The peak of his cap had been cut either side so that the peak came flat above his nose, just like the guards. But what fascinated me was his size. He couldn't have been much more than 5ft 2in, but he had the voice of a 6-footer! 'You don't bloody move until I tell you to move!' he bellowed again. 'In fact,' he screeched, 'you don't bloody do anything for the next six weeks unless I tell you to do it, do you understand?' He took in a deep breath, then made the coach windows rattle loudly by yelling out, 'When I say do you understand, you all reply by shouting back "yes, Corporal". Now,' he screamed, 'let's have a practice run: do you *understand*?!' 'Yes, Corporal,' we shouted back loudly. 'And again!' he shrieked. 'Yes, Corporal!' we yelled in blind panic. I reckon we must have screamed at least a dozen 'Yes, Corporals!' before he even let us off the bloody coach. Okay, I thought, I had been a naughty boy in the past and experienced some nasty Borstals and remand homes. So this was about the same. Keep your nose clean, don't get noticed and keep your head down below the parapet. Don't be the wise guy or he'll dig you out as an example in front of all the other blokes in the flight.

Eventually, we all followed him up a paved path, lined by small rocks – all painted white by toothbrushes, as I was later told – into a Nissen hut that would be our home for the next six weeks. The hut had a gleaming, polished floor – almost like a mirror, as it actually reflected your shadow. In the centre there was this huge black stove that had been lovingly burnished by many unwilling hands over a long period of time. The bed spaces, all highly polished, were allocated by our corporal, and I was lucky enough to get the end one next to the partition that housed his private room. I say 'lucky' because I only had one person beside me rather than two. So instead of a snorer either side, I only had possible aggro on one side to contend with. We were forced to stand to attention for ages while this jumped-up

'By the right, quick march!' *(RAF Museum, Hendon)*

It's a long way home from Hednesford. *(Author's collection)*

little martinet read the itinerary from his list. This included the time we would have to get up in the mornings, as well as the time we would eat and the times for drill, for kit inspections, for target practice on the range and for the dreaded assault course. There would be no leave for anyone until we had completed the six-week course. 'Any questions?' he barked loudly. 'No, Corporal!' we all yelled back in unison. I thought I detected a half-smile on his face as we shouted back. He knew from past experience that he had put his mark on us and for the next six weeks his authority wouldn't be challenged. 'Right,' he yelled. 'Flight dismissed and get your kit stowed away. Get your mug and irons at the ready, 'cos grub will be served in one hour.' With that he executed a smart about-turn and marched off to his room, his gleaming boots clicking almost musically on the gleaming floor. His door slammed shut and we were at peace for the next hour or so.

The lads just sat on their bunks in stony silence for what seemed like an age. I've heard of front-line troops suffering shell-shock in the heat of battle, but I reckon we all had 'Drill Corporal shell-shock' – and we'd only just arrived on camp! Apart from that plonker Nige, I didn't know any of the others in our hut. I had a quick look round just to see who I'd been lumbered with for the next six weeks of hell. They certainly were a motley crew, but I took it upon myself to liven up the proceedings and suggested that it was an appropriate time to introduce ourselves to each other. A few of the lads were genuine cockneys like myself, and as time went on we became good mates for the rest of our training. What fascinated me from the off was the immediate and instinctive nicknaming. The tallest guy in the billet became 'Lofty', while the smallest guy became 'Little Chas'. Anyone called White became 'Chalky', and all the Smiths were 'Smudgers'. The Clarks all became 'Nobby' and the Murphys all became 'Spud'. As for me, I had rather a prominent head so I was given the nickname of 'Nutty'! And so it went on, almost like an ageless tribal ritual. One poor guy, who had been studying at a theological college to become a priest, became the butt of our somewhat cruel and hurtful humour. He was rather portly, with a podgy face, ginger hair and an almost basin-like 'Friar Tuck' haircut. He was a really nice guy and he loved Jesus to bits. So, straightaway, his nickname became 'The Vicar'. He really shouldn't have been in the company of such philistines as us. I felt dreadfully sorry for him at the completion of our basic training when our postings eventually came through. He was desperate to continue his mission for Jesus and wanted to become a padre in the RAF.

This was where the practice in the RAF of putting square pegs into round holes really came to the fore. The world's worst posting, as we found out as time went by, was to the RAF Regiment in Dundee. The RAF Regiment were basically the guards of the RAF, who protected the airfields and manned the ack-ack guns. In effect, they were the 'Army' of the RAF. We were told that the Regiment had loads of drill and plenty of bull, and that if you were a born skiver like myself you should stay well clear of this mob! But, would you believe it, the Vicar drew the short straw and got a posting to the RAF Regiment in Dundee! I remember he cried constantly for days after hearing the ghastly news. I sincerely hope his saviour helped him to survive that ordeal and, who knows, with his undying faith he may well have become the 'Bishop' of Dundee!

Having read numerous books about the Battle of Britain and the heroics of the fighter pilots, I was quite 'genned up', as they say in the RAF, about the line-up and formation of the aircrews. So, it amazed me to discover that this line-up was exactly the same for the ground staff, even for us new recruits. The top dog in charge of an RAF station was a group captain. The rest of the camp was divided into wings, each with a wing commander. Then each wing was divided into squadrons, with the squadron leaders in charge. Finally, the squadrons were all split up into flights and a flight lieutenant was in charge of each flight. If my memory serves me right, I think we were in G Flight, B Wing. This had the immediate effect of bringing competition into our training, almost like the different houses at public schools and universities. We were told from day one by our flight 'looie', when he spoke to us in our hut, that he wanted our flight to be the best on the passing-out parade. And if one of us could manage to win the

Top brass on the saluting base. *(RAF Museum, Hendon)*

coveted Sword of Honour, as the best recruit, it would be a big feather in his cap. Unfortunately for him, we were a shambles even on the passing-out parade. So, he had to try his luck with the next intake!

We were taught anything and everything by our drill corporal. How to make our beds ready for inspection and how to 'square-off' all our kit on our wardrobe shelves. I never thought I'd see the day when I was actually cutting up pieces of cardboard to help accentuate the squaring-off look! He also showed us how to burn the pimples off our boots with a red-hot spoon, then how to use the same red-hot spoon to lovingly apply the black polish with plenty of spit that eventually made the boots absolutely gleaming. He taught us how to march in step, how to 'right-dress' and how to drill with a rifle. My mind was a confused flurry of 'one, two' and

Appearance was everything: Brasso, blanco and bags of bull. We used soap inside the creases of our trousers to give them a knife-sharp edge. *(RAF Museum, Hendon)*

The two drill corporals at Hednesford who made our lives a misery for six weeks. *(Author's collection)*

'left, right, left' and 'herbout turn', 'right-dress' and 'slope h'arms' and 'pree-sent h'arms', ending with the inevitable scream of, 'You're a bloody shambles, the lot of you!' Without realising it, we were slowly becoming institutionalised, almost like being in hospital for a long period or even in the nick! If one of us didn't get it right, whatever 'it' might be, we were told that it would always reflect badly on the rest of the flight, then our drill corporal, our flight looie and right through to our wing commander. That's what we were told, anyway! But this age-old ritual really worked and had the immediate effect of making us all work together as a team.

Our drill corporal would still do his nut if things didn't go exactly right at the first try. But even I could perceive that this shower and rabble that was G Flight was actually looking pretty good on the parade ground. Apart from the Vicar, who had terrible trouble sorting out his right from his left and was absolutely hopeless at counting paces, we were beginning to look the business. At the risk of losing face among my gang of North London yobbos, I was actually enjoying the experience of square-bashing; in fact, I was quite good at it. So good, in fact, that one day our corporal allowed me to drill the flight, while he sat down and had a fag. Call me an old poser if you will, but I quite enjoyed the feeling of controlling a group of men and getting them to 'leave on the left, quick march'. Then, a loud command to bring them back with an 'about-turn' and, finally, a bellowing 'Halt!' to end my solo performance. Our corporal tried to chat me into signing on for five years. He indicated that I had the makings of a drill corporal. But not me – no way!

I really should have known better when he 'sweet-talked' me one day. With the benefit of hindsight, the drill corporals probably pick out one recruit from each intake whom they believe to have a strong influence over the others and whom they can manipulate to their own advantage. And this time around it was little ol' me – plenty of cockney chat, bags of confidence, popular with the lads and always good for a giggle. The corporal called me into his room one day, asked me to sit down and enquired, did I want a cup of tea or a fag? Then came the old chestnut that he'd probably used for donkey's years. 'I've got a small money problem,' he said rather sadly, 'and I'm hoping you and the boys can help me out until I get straight.' It was like taking candy from a baby. I took the bait hook, line and sinker. After all, this was my mentor and my drill corporal! 'Wot, you want me to get a whip-round going among the lads,

Instructing staff at a school of recruit training 'somewhere in England'. Don't be fooled by a smiling drill corporal! *(RAF Museum, Hendon)*

Corp?' I responded gullibly. 'No, no, nothing like that,' he replied, knowing full well that was against Queen's Regulations and a punishable offence. He went across the room to his locker and pulled out a watch. 'My old Dad gave me this,' he said, holding up the watch with tears in his eyes. 'But,' he sniffed, rather too loudly I thought, 'I need to get rid of it to raise some money and I'd like you to raffle it among the lads, 'cos I'm desperate to get straight.' Come on, be fair. I was only eighteen and this guy was like a god to our flight.

I believed him implicitly and worked my socks off selling the raffle tickets to the whole hut. One for all and all for one, that was the slogan. Suddenly, one of the guys said he wasn't going to buy a raffle ticket. His Dad, an ex-professional soldier, told him it was always a fiddle. Me and the boys were livid. This one guy was putting us all in Queer Street because of his stupid old Dad. He was eventually coerced into buying a ticket as a gesture of solidarity! Even when I found out the eventual outcome of the raffle, I still didn't tumble that it was a regular, six-week scam. I drew the raffle, with all the lads clustered around, and a big cheer went up when Chalky White had the winning ticket. He went into the corporal's room and was told that unfortunately the raffle didn't cover the value of the watch, but the corporal was happy to give him about one pound, I think, because he was the winner. I was absolutely fuming. I had spent hours of my time collecting about four quid or more from the boys. Yet this little arse-hole had blatantly taken the piss out of me by giving the winner a measly pound! So he was three quid in front and I had finished with zilch! That's another lesson I learned early in life: people will use you if you appear just a little gullible. However, that still made me top dog in the flight and I was just a little bit more cunning than this liberty-taker had bargained for. He knew that I knew that he had pulled a diabolical stroke, using me as the fall guy. But unlike the other mugs he had used in the past, corporal or not, he didn't scare me.

Soon after the dodgy raffle, I stormed into his room and told him in no uncertain terms that I'd blow the whistle on him if he ever took the piss out of me again. He didn't say a word! I indicated a few weeks later that I wasn't fit enough to attempt the dreadful assault course, but I didn't want to mention the dodgy raffle if he decided to send me to the medic. It was his turn to have the squeeze put on him. He didn't like it one little bit, but he had to lump it! So, on the day of the dreaded assault course my 'punishment' was to sit in the hut and polish my boots. That was tough! When all my mates returned to our hut, covered from head to foot in mud, shit and grime, and collapsed moaning on their bunks, I was forced to give some loud coughs, hold my stomach and wipe my feverish brow. I don't really think the subterfuge worked, if the looks I got from the lads were anything to go by!

Towards the end of basic training, we were told by our corporal that very soon we needed to decide what section of the RAF we'd like to join for the rest of our service. You could train as an aircraft fitter, or, Nige's favourite, the Radar Unit or Signals Unit. You could apply for an officer's training course at Cranwell, or take a Physical Training Course and become a PTI. In fact, apart from the rigours of the RAF Regiment in Dundee, all the courses seemed to be quite interesting. But I had a one-track mind. I desperately needed a posting near home to further my football career. I had been loaned out to a Southern League club during my national service and was on three quid a match, but only if I could make it on Saturdays. This was exactly twice as much as I got in weekly wages from the RAF, and coupled with a one-pound win bonus and half a quid for a draw would make me very well off! That's when my being sent to Hednesford, although it wasn't my choice in the first place, turned out lucky for me.

When I was eventually ushered in to see the officer in charge of postings, he immediately asked me what club I played for. Now I knew he had been peeking at my form and seen the words 'pro footballer'. It turned out that he was one of a group of officers who made sure that any professional sportsperson was posted to the station that specialised in their particular sport. The camp at Uxbridge, just at the end of the Piccadilly tube line, was the home of the very successful Bomber Command football team, so he suggested Uxbridge to me. This sounded perfect for weekends, playing footie for really good money. But, as always, there was a catch. I would be posted first to the ADU, the Advanced Drill Unit, to be renamed in 1960 as the Queen's Colour Squadron. You've probably seen their displays at all the big military functions – even the Commonwealth Games in Manchester. Their drill is good, very good. These special sports postings were a bit like the internal RAF Mafia. If the group captain in charge of a camp had a passion for a particular sport and wanted his team to whack all the other camps, the posting officers would do their best to oblige the 'groupies'. Any favour would be noted and duly repaid later in their careers! A bit like the situation facing the son of one of my mates recently. He was on the shortlist for a good job in a merchant bank in the City. Unfortunately, all the other applicants had far better qualifications than him. However, my mate, a fellow golfer, knew that the manager was an absolute golf nut, living and breathing for his beloved golf team at the bank and wanting them to whack all the other banks. So, when the son, prompted by his Dad beforehand, of course, just happened to tell the manager at the interview that he was in fact a single-figure handicapper and had played county golf, surprise surprise, he got the job without the guy even bothering to check his CV!

The conditions of my posting to Uxbridge were spelt out to me in a complicated manner. I knew what the officer was saying, even if I could

Queen Juliana of the Netherlands inspects. *(RAF Museum, Hendon)*

never prove that he'd said it. In essence it was this. I would have to endure the drill and the bullshit of the ADU for a short while. But if I made it to the Bomber Command team, I could expect a nice cushy number down at the sports store for the rest of my service. It sounded good to me. I was very confident of my ability to make the team, so I signed on the dotted line. Even after more than fifty years down the line, I still cringe at my youthful impetuosity at that time. It stands to reason that if intricate and devious plans had been hatched to get *all* the pro footballers to Uxbridge from just about every training camp in the UK, these plans must include the 'disposal' of all those many individuals who didn't make it to the final squad! There'll be lots more about that in the chapter about my time in Uxbridge.

Meanwhile, G Flight was working well. We had about two weeks to go before the final passing-out parade. But many of the lads, myself included,

Nearing the end of basic training. *(RAF Museum, Hendon)*

were getting bored of staying in the camp and were looking for a bit of action. So we got involved in a punch-up just for visiting a different NAAFI on the camp. It turned out that we recruits had to stick to our own NAAFI and not enter the one used by all the permanent airmen stationed there. I made what I considered a valid point: we were all in the same RAF and why couldn't we use a different NAAFI if we wanted to? Anyway, not only did I get a couple of right-handers for my cheek, I also got a roasting from our flight looie for being off limits. Luckily, the following weekend our corporal announced that our flight would be given a break and allowed a day pass to visit the local town. If my memory serves me right, I believe the town was Cannock. It doesn't take the Brain of Britain to work out how we spent our day in Cannock. For sure, Cannock is probably a very pretty town, but the pubs are even prettier! Can't you just

Parades . . . *(RAF Museum, Hendon)*

envisage the scenario? We were vibrant young men who had been banged up as if we'd been in the nick, then hassled by a 'poisoned dwarf' for over a month. Now was the time to let our hair down. Sadly, like most vibrant young men who had been banged up we went over the top and by the time we got on the bus back to the camp I was absolutely legless.

Even to this day I still haven't got a clue what I said or who I insulted in my drunken stupor. All I can remember is squaring up to some Jock airmen on wasteground outside the camp. They were calling me – among many other choice things – a foul-mouthed English bastard who needed to wash his mouth out. Suffice to say, I had the shit beaten out of me. In fact, I've still got the Scottish teethmarks on my left forearm after more than fifty years! So my mates helped to guide this bruised and battered drunk back to his quarters and I crashed out totally oblivious to the world. Come Monday, my cuts and bruises weren't too painful. But my testicles,

. . . and more parades. *(RAF Museum, Hendon)*

which had received a severe kicking, were throbbing like mad! Our corporal knew the score and he was enjoying it, having heard the news on the grapevine. But no way was I going to report sick and have to explain the reasons for my injuries. So I soldiered on with my drill, looking for all the world like Groucho Marx doing his silly walk!

For the final two weeks before the passing-out parade, we were drilling every day. On one of our very rare days off we would spend most of the time cleaning our equipment and readying ourselves for the kit inspection the following morning. Why on earth we should be pulling a lump of rag called a 'four by two' through the barrel of a rifle, God only knows! Once again I had told our corporal I was 'sick' and I'd missed the day when the lads had been up the rifle range firing at targets, so I'd never even fired a bloody gun! We were up bright and early the next morning, washed, shaved and dressed and fussing around with our kit ready for the

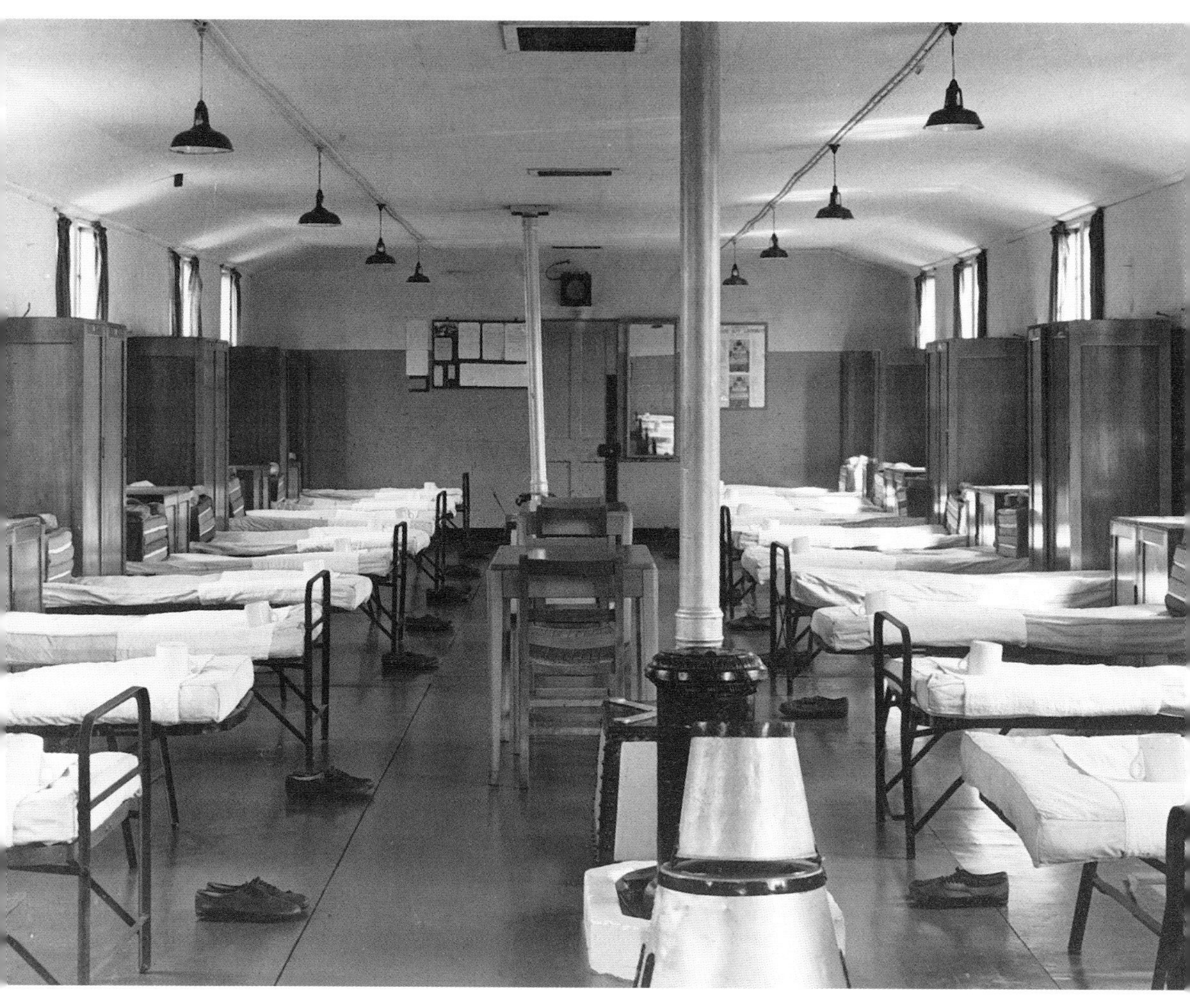

G Flight's quarters at training camp for the six weeks – all sterile and clinical! *(Author's collection)*

inspection. A bark from our corporal of 'Atten-shun!' indicated the arrival of the flight looie and the warrant officer, carrying his clipboard under his arm. The flight looie told us to 'stand at ease' and went through the motions of trying to look interested as he moved slowly down the hut, moving his eyes from one side to the other. He was closely followed by the warrant officer and our corporal. But, in all honesty, our officer looked pissed off with the whole affair and only stopped a couple of times to say something to one of the lads in a quiet voice. The warrant officer, a really large man with an even larger belly and a prominent moustache, then proceeded to write something down on his clipboard. The fat man looked as though he'd like to fill up *all* of his clipboard with names! Thankfully, by the time they reached my kit and my bedspace the officer had had enough and couldn't wait to leave. So it was 'Atten-shun!', salutes all round and the two of them departed. I believe a couple of the lads got a minor bollocking for an untidy kit layout.

All we had to do now was keep our noses clean, concentrate on our drill, and look forward to leaving this dump and enjoying a week's leave at home. But Sod's Law being what it is, that's never as simple as it sounds. As they say in showbiz, it ain't over 'til the fat lady sings!

The Passing-out Parade

After six long weeks of real hard graft G Flight was looking the business and a real outfit. We were performing well on the parade ground with our drill – so well, in fact, that our corporal had even taught us how to drill using just numbers instead of the normal commands. So we would start

We had practice after practice before the passing-out parade. Our boots must have worn grooves in the concrete. *(RAF Museum, Hendon)*

It seemed like the inspection would never end. I was busting for a pee! *(RAF Museum, Hendon)*

with the command, 'Leave on the left, quick march.' Then we would count fifty paces, and after a count of 'one pause, two pause and three', we would all do an about-turn in unison. Next, another count of fifty paces and all halt together. Then, count to five and all left face. Yet another count to five and present arms. Count to five again and order arms. Finally, count to five and stand at ease. It was pretty simple but very impressive if all the guys were working as a team, and I thoroughly enjoyed the experience. Later on with the Advanced Drill Unit at Uxbridge, I would learn to drill like that with no commands for up to fifteen minutes!

The one fly in the ointment was the Vicar, who simply didn't know his right foot from his left and had a counting system all of his own. G Flight would curl up with laughter and our drill corporal would go ballistic as the Vicar eventually joined us, all hot and sweaty at our stand-at-ease position. God only knows where he had been on the parade ground! Our corporal was starting to sweat blood over the Vicar; just one guy like him cocking it up on the big day could destroy six weeks of hard graft for the whole flight. So I had a quiet chat with our nervous leader after one of our drill sessions and assured him that the Vicar wouldn't be a problem at the passing-out parade. 'What we'll do, Corp, is bury him in the middle of the flight,' I said, 'then with one of the lads on either side of him, they'll be able to almost lift him up and steer him around the parade ground – a bit like a ventriloquist's dummy!' He just grunted nervously and said he'd have my balls if it went pear-shaped and cost him his job!

After all the practice, woe betide the poor sod who passed out on parade. *(RAF Museum, Hendon)*

The big day for the recruits was fast approaching, and our corporal now seemed much more friendly and helpful! He spent many hours checking our equipment for the passing-out parade and trained me incessantly for my important role as right marker. In effect, the rest of the flight took their dressing and their paces from the right marker. An additional face suddenly appeared on the parade ground to help our corporal brush up our final drill. This man was introduced to us as 'Corporal Spence', and he was an absolute drill maniac. Often it would be getting dark by the time we headed back to our quarters. The guy was totally possessed, taller than our man, but still with the peak of his hat flat to his nose. But what a nose! I've heard of 'beaked noses', but I reckon this guy could peck you to death at two paces! He had one of those baby faces that had hardly ever grown stubble – but never be taken in by appearances. This guy was a hard taskmaster and quite brutal in his methods. None of the guys was ever completely safe from Corporal Spence, and the guys who weren't that hot at drill suffered most of the tongue-lashing every day.

That completes the 'circle' and brings me neatly back to the poor old Vicar. He was having a terrible time under the new taskmaster, and I was getting a little concerned about his health and welfare. So concerned, in fact, that I told our corporal that he could well have a potential suicide on his hands unless Corporal Spence laid off the constant bullying for a while. That was enough to make his eyes bulge in blind panic as he suddenly visualised the possible consequences of banner headlines in the press: 'National Serviceman Bullied Into Committing Suicide'. That would certainly have ruined him and his RAF pension! Things finally got back to normal after that, minus Corporal Spence.

Our corporal's job was now on the line, and if we cocked it up on the big day then his RAF career would be finished. He repeatedly bashed our ears day after day before the big event about the line-up of the parade, the dignitaries who would be present and where they would be sitting. He would address us in an almost paternal way as we sat around in our hut, as though we were Boy Scouts. 'I just want you to relax, lads, and try and enjoy what you've been taught,' he'd say. 'Remember to keep one eye on your markers and just march in step with the band.' Then he'd express his real fears by puffing feverishly on his ciggie while saying almost nonchalantly, 'I don't give a monkey's if we don't come first, second or third among the four Flights. But please, lads, not last, please.'

We are starting to look the business at Hednesford! *(Author's collection)*

Finally, the big day arrived. It was rather sad for me, as all the suburban mums and dads were there to see their boys pass out, but not my parents – I guess they couldn't afford the train fare. But I was an important right marker and, parents or not, I was determined not to let all my mates down. G Flight all gathered outside the Nissen hut, our home for the past six weeks. Most of us had stayed up late into the night to give our kit the final once-over. There'd been lots of spitting and polishing of boots; waiting your turn to use the solitary iron to press your uniform; polishing badges; and putting white blanco on our webbing belts.We certainly looked the part and the white webbing-belts gave off an almost eerie glow in the early morning light. Our corporal was fussing around like a mother hen, checking this and checking that and getting his knickers in a twist. Then we were stood to attention at the arrival of our flight looie. Surprise surprise, it was a new face. This was intriguing, as it was certainly not the

I still get a shiver down my spine when I hear 'The Royal Air Force March Past' played by a military band. *(RAF Museum, Hendon)*

norm to change flight looies before the final day. This guy really looked the business in his dress uniform, with a big ceremonial sword hanging down by his side. But he wasn't at all like all the other young officers, still wet behind the ears. For starters, he was six or seven years older and, more to the point, he had pilot's wings displayed on his chest. We all wondered, what on earth was a qualified pilot doing in a God-awful dump like this? The whisper on the grapevine later on from the drill corporals was that this fella was a bit of a rascal and a ladies' man. Rumour had it that this was a punishment posting for him because he had been caught rumping the wife of a very senior officer! But I liked his laid-back approach and his obvious dislike for all the bullshit. Yet, strangely, even he sounded rather nervous as he gave us our pre-passing-out pep-talk in a soft, refined voice. 'Gentlemen,' he said, 'do your best out there today, and if you happen to be the top flight that indeed would be a bonus for me.' He paused, then with a twinkle in his eye added, 'In fact, if you did come out on top it could mean my ticket out of this bloody dump.' Finally, a loud command of 'Atten-shun!' Our corporal saluted him and he was gone.

One of the lads whispered to me, 'How d'ya fancy G Flight for a half-a-quid bet, Alf?' I smiled and replied, 'No way, mate, not even at a hundred to one!' We still had to solve the problem of the Vicar, who didn't know his left from his right. On top of that he was really suffering from a severe attack of nerves and sweating like a pig. His ginger hair was dripping wet and he kept wiping his big chubby face in a theatrical manner – almost like a thespian after a long spell on stage! The original game plan of burying him in the middle of the flight and hoping that nobody would notice him doing his own thing needed reviewing. I had a word with our corporal and we decided to put the two tallest guys either side of him, so in effect nobody could even see him. But despite our intricate plans the Vicar was worrying everybody.

At long last we all gathered on the parade ground. The sun was just coming out, but it was still chilly. But better to have it chilly than all hot and sweaty. I was able to have a quick look round at all the spectators. The dais was reserved for our group captain, who was the station commander, and all the visiting dignitaries. I noticed the local mayor sitting there, wearing his chain of office. I chuckled to myself and thought, he's probably only come for the free booze! After lots of shuffling around and barking orders of 'right dress', we finally got the order of 'by the left, quick march', and we all followed the band in formation. I've always enjoyed the sound of marching bands, and even after more than forty years of driving a London cab and having seen the Changing of the Guard at Buckingham Palace hundreds of times I still get a buzz when the police hold up the traffic and the band marches by me, followed by the impressive guards.

Strange to say, the passing-out parade went pretty well. We all executed a smart 'eyes right' as we marched past the groupie and all the dignitaries on the dais. The group captain, looking absolutely resplendent in his dress uniform with the impressive 'scrambled egg' on his hat, saluted us as we marched past. We marched up to the end of the parade ground, did a smart about-turn, then marched back to the dais and this time it was 'eyes left' on our way past. Another about-turn and back to the dais again. Then we were halted and ordered to 'right face', followed by lots more shuffling around at the order to 'right dress'. Then, it was 'slope h'arms' and 'h'order h'arms' and finally 'pree-sent h'arms'. The CO took the salute and the crowd clapped politely as we all marched off – and suddenly the six weeks of bull were well and truly over and a new way of life was beckoning.

We were like a bunch of excited schoolkids when we finally got back to our Nissen hut. We hadn't been a disaster and we hadn't embarrassed ourselves or our corporal. Even the Vicar was looking pretty chuffed with himself. He had probably done his own thing, but nobody had even

The rabble that was G Flight at Hednesford Training Camp; I wonder where they all are now? The author is third from right on the front row. *(Author's collection)*

noticed him doing it. So our well-thought-out game plan had worked a treat. In essence, though, it was a bit of an anticlimax and a sudden and abrupt end to our way of life for the past six weeks. Even our drill corporal was different – he was almost human! True, our flight hadn't come first on the passing-out parade so the randy flight looie still didn't have a ticket out of this dump. But more importantly for our corporal, we hadn't come last. He had done enough with this latest bunch of no-hopers to survive another intake and continue with his lucrative scams and fiddles. But what a drastic change had suddenly come over him – talk about Jekyll and Hyde! He was sucking up to the very people he'd been slagging off for the past six weeks. After a couple of beers back at our hut, he began hugging us and drunkenly calling us 'mates' and offering to sign our photos. I think I preferred him as a jumped-up little despot with a foul mouth. But, hey, let's be fair – he was only letting his hair down after six arduous weeks of licking us into shape.

Our very last night in that particular NAAFI was rowdy to say the least! Each and every one of us was on a high. Okay, so completing six weeks' square-bashing wasn't exactly rocket science. But in all honesty, we were only overgrown kids in uniform and every man Jack of us was over the moon and tickled pink that we had cracked it! The beer was flowing like wine and some of the suburban lads were beginning to look the worse for wear. Us cockney boys were sinking pints as though we had hollow legs, with seemingly no ill effects. How that all changed dramatically when they eventually closed the bar and we went to stand up! Imagine my surprise and horror to discover it was the plonker Nige who had half carried me back to our quarters. Once again we were all in the same boat and had got through the 'voyage' without sinking or drowning.

Then suddenly, and almost without warning, my life at Hednesford was well and truly over. We said our tearful goodbyes, yet in all honesty these were crocodile tears! But although we hated the godforsaken dump, we had all suffered it as a band of brothers. We had all incurred the wrath of our corporal at one time or another and been given demeaning tasks as punishment. So what if you had to put white paint on the big, round stones outside our hut every day for a week, and with a toothbrush? And who gave a toss if you were told to blacken and polish the stove in the middle of our hut, instead of going down to the cookhouse for dinner with all the rest of the boys?

Suffice to say, with all my chat and my track record of giving the corporal some lip, I had been lumbered with these soppy chores on a regular basis. But it hadn't bothered me one little bit. I used gaily to slap the black polish all over the stove and pretend it was the corporal's ugly 'boat race'. Then I'd say in a loud voice, as of course he was nowhere around at the time, 'I hope you get run over by a tank, you effing little poisoned dwarf!' But what *had* got right up my nose was the way this little despot enjoyed taking diabolical liberties with the Vicar. Okay, so I suffered my demeaning chores in silence because I was out of order. But he wouldn't have dared to treat me the way he treated the Vicar because I would have given him a smack on the chops and suffered the consequences! The Vicar was a lovely bloke, but he was very podgy, unfit and totally unsuited to any kind of strenuous sporting activity. So the poisoned dwarf took great delight in making him run around the parade ground with his rifle above his head, simply because he had no coordination and couldn't keep in step with the rest of us! I could never forgive him for that sort of bullying.

Strange to say, I have never seen a single one of the guys in our flight for over fifty years, other than when it was my misfortune to get lumbered with Nige some way down the line in my service. And dear old Lofty – I believe his name was Don – became a copper in the Metropolitan Police and, much to my chagrin, actually nicked me for jumping the lights in Tottenham Court Road in my taxi! But he was with another copper and that was his job. And we had a nice chat about the good old days while he wrote out the ticket. I often think about all the other guys in our hut, who, like me, are now pushing three score years and ten. How many of them are still alive and kicking? What about Little Chas, or Smudger or Chalky? Have they all enjoyed a happy contented life as I have, with a lovely wife, kids and lots of grandchildren? And how about the dear old Vicar? Did he survive the rigours of the RAF Regiment and find his salvation in a country parish? Or maybe he reached the dizzy height of bishopric! Just working on simple statistics, the odds are that of all those guys with whom I shared my life for some six weeks in the early 1950s quite a few must have passed away in the ensuing years, while many others perhaps have endured unhappy lives with broken marriages, bad health and the like. These are some of the thoughts that bug me constantly. Maybe when this book is published some of my former room-mates of G Flight,

RAF Hednesford in the mid-1950s might get in touch with me and tell me about their lives over the past fifty-odd years.

Anyway, we all went to our different homes for a week's leave before moving on to our postings to every RAF station in the UK – and the world. I think some of the guys went overseas, to places like Germany and Singapore. Maybe some of them drew the short straw and were unlucky enough to finish up in Korea.

The train journey back to London felt really weird. Just a couple of short months before – though it felt like a lifetime ago – I had been heading north as a civvy, feeling really nervous and, dare I say it, missing my Mum like mad. Now I was a fully fledged member of the RAF in full uniform, albeit an aircraftman second class, the very lowest of ranks! Out of the original trainload of anxious teenagers heading into the unknown some two months before, there were only half a dozen going home on this particular train. Most of the others had been shipped to the other RAF training camps all over England and were probably now heading for London like me. I couldn't help but notice Nige – you could hear him a mile away, laughing and joking with his suburban gang! Unusually for me, I was very quiet and thoughtful, reflecting on my future in the RAF.

That more or less closed the book on Hednesford. But not for me, as I am blessed, or maybe cursed, with a retentive memory, and even after more than half a century I can still close my eyes and recall every day at that dump. I can clearly visualise all the fresh young faces in our hut and detect the fear they were desperately trying to hide – especially some of the suburban lads who found it really hard going. And whether I liked it or not, my painful experiences, first as an evacuee during the Second World War and then during my spell in Borstal, had hardened me. So in all honesty, a foul-mouthed malevolent midget screaming expletives at us hadn't bothered me one iota. To give him his due, though, the poisoned dwarf was a very good judge of character and he knew immediately whom to dig out and bully and whose lives to make a living hell. He and I had had an unwritten agreement from day one. Nothing was ever said and he certainly didn't do me any favours at any time. But my somewhat presumptuous title of 'professional footballer' and possession of a strong personality had made me a natural leader among the other virgin young airmen. He'd already marked me down in his mind as somebody who could be very useful to him, both as a middle-man in any negotiations with the flight and for getting support for one of his many scams! I hadn't minded getting involved in his fiddles if I'd got a bit of the proceeds, but I certainly wasn't going to do it for nowt. That's why after the crooked raffle fiasco I'd marched into his room, slammed the door and told him in no uncertain terms that he couldn't take the piss out of me and get away with it. 'I ain't doing any more of your shit scams,' I had told him angrily, 'and if you give me any more grief for the rest of my time at this piss-'ole, I'll blow the effing whistle on you.' Funny, that – I didn't do too much of anything for the rest of my stay, yet we became almost friends!

And, yes, even though I had been deservedly beaten up by a couple of Jocks when I was legless and foul-mouthed, most of the lads still looked up to me. I suppose I was a larger-than-life character, seldom seen in suburbia! The Hednesford experience was only a split second in the context of a lifetime, but a treasured episode that will remain in my memory to the end of my days. I can only hope and pray that most of my mates who shared the hardships and pain with me are living long, fruitful and contented lives.

CHAPTER THREE

ANOTHER LIFE AT UXBRIDGE

After six long weeks of bullshit, being told what to do and when to do it by a malevolent midget, I'm sorry to say my week's leave turned into a glorified pub-crawl. Some of my mates who were on the run even came out of hiding to celebrate with me. I remember one night we were all absolutely legless in one of the many pubs up Caledonian Road. Unfortunately, the guv'nor called 'Time!' and threw us all out before I'd had the opportunity to relieve myself. So in a drunken stupor, I proceeded to do just that against the pub wall. Suddenly, a light was shone on me and a loud, gruff voice shouted in anger, ''Allo, 'allo, wot 'ave we got 'ere?' I stared bleary eyed and unsteadily past the light and, even though I was legless, I knew the voice belonged to a copper. Now I was for it. It was time for my natural cockney cunning to get me off the hook, and I apologise from the bottom of my heart to all those brave guys I tried to impersonate. 'I'm shorry, officer,' I slurred, 'but I'm 'ome on leave and I've 'ad a rough time over there.'

The burly copper came nearer to get a better look at me, and it was plain for him to see by my shorn head that I was in the forces. 'You been out there, lad?' he asked sympathetically. I nodded drunkenly. Nobody even mentioned the name of any country, but I knew full well he meant Korea. 'I was a regular in the Guards,' he said wistfully, 'and you boys in the Glosters did a bleedin' brilliant job at the Imjin River.' He patted me on the back of the head in a fatherly way and said, 'On your way, son, and behave yourself.' Then he was gone, and by a miracle I hadn't got nicked. I've carried the guilt of that encounter right through my life. The Glorious Glosters really did fight a brave battle at the Imjin River against overwhelming odds. I'm very sorry that I used their name in vain.

Suddenly, my week's leave was up and it was time to move out. So I got all of my gear together, said goodbye to my family and set off for King's Cross by walking down Caledonian Road. Yet again I was confronted by the 'Korean' experience. This old guy came up to me, shook my hand warmly and said, with tears in his eyes, 'Good luck, son, look after yourself, it will soon be all over.' I had tears in my eyes when I replied, but these were tears of laughter. How could I possibly tell the old fella that my destination was at the end of the Piccadilly tube line? So I said gruffly and with feeling, as they say on stage, 'Thanks, Pop, we'll keep 'em out of Blighty.' Then I marched off smartly in my hobnailed boots, before bursting into uncontrollable laughter!

We Brits really are a funny lot. Give us a war or a conflict anywhere on the globe, and we suddenly revert to the siege mentality of the Second World War. This old fella was probably in the process of refurbishing his Anderson shelter ready to repel the bombs from the Korean planes! The geographical whereabouts of other countries has never been our strongpoint. Take my old Dad, for instance. He did his time in the Duke of Cornwall's Light Infantry between the wars and spent much of his service in Egypt. Try as I might, all during my week's leave, I couldn't convince him that the Koreans definitely weren't after the Suez Canal! President Nasser, maybe; but the Koreans, no! My Dad was from the old generation of out-and-out bigots and racists. And, sadly, if my son hadn't fallen in love and married a gorgeous black girl from Surinam – formerly Dutch Guyana – I would probably have passed my bigotry on to the next generation. My old Dad had a simple and quite unworkable formula when it came to colour. If the individuals happened to be black, according to him, they were 'Johnnies', an old derogatory Army slang term like 'Wogs'.

However, his problems arose when it came to having to differentiate between the nearly black, the nearly white and the not-so-black and the not-so-white, not unlike the major problem that faced the South African government in the 1970s and '80s when they were desperately trying to categorise their population in line with their racist policies of Apartheid. The millions of kids from mixed marriages, some half-Bantu, some half-Indian and many half-Asian, became a headache for the authorities. So, like all 'good' zealous bigots, they conveniently labelled all these millions of kids, instantly making them second-class citizens and euphemistically calling them 'Cape Coloureds'. Mind you, our black citizens didn't fare much better in the UK during the 1950s and '60s – especially after the *Empire Windrush* docked in Southampton full to the brim with families from the Caribbean, who had answered the call from the then Tory government of the day for menial manpower. These people had forsaken their island paradises in the hope of finding a better life in the 'mother country'. Yet, what they encountered was an institutionalised racist and bigoted country, with ex-Cabinet Minister Enoch Powell making his inflammatory 'Rivers of Blood' speech, which was probably the making of the National Front. I distinctly remember the 'To Let' signs hanging in the windows of the scruffy houses around Notting Hill at the time, many of these properties owned by the notorious landlord Peter Rachman. They read, 'No Blacks, No Irish'; and even that long ago I recall I was shocked that these people could get away with such blatant racism. But we London cabbies can always think up a joke in adversity, and the guys used to say when commenting on the 'To Let' signs: 'What about the poor old black Paddy, he must be a million to one to find a place to live?'

But back to my old Dad, allow me to explain. My eldest sister was having a romantic fling with this local guy called Philip, whose family hailed from Liverpool. He used to take my Dad out to the pub regularly and ply him with plenty of free booze. I remember my old Dad thought he was the cat's whiskers. So when Philip asked him round to meet his Mum and Dad, with a view to a possible engagement, my Dad was thrilled to bits and proudly told us all beforehand, 'Philip is a lovely geezer and will make a good husband for my daughter.' Wow-ee, what a sudden change of heart when he returned from his visit to the parents. But even though my Dad was a dyed-in-the-wool racist and a bigot, he was still my Dad and, strange to say, I felt sorry for him. He seemed to be almost in a trance and very distant. 'So,' said I, 'how did the visit go, Dad?' I could see then he was white with rage and his voice was shaking as he snarled back in anger. 'How did the visit go, Dad?' he said, mimicking me. 'I'll tell you how the bleedin' visit went,' he snapped. 'His ol' man is as black as the bleedin' Ace of Spades and no daughter of mine is gonna marry any son of a Johnnie, and that's the end of it.' I had been taught bigotry and racism by my old Dad, but I still had an enquiring mind and a sense of fair play. So, at the risk of copping a right-hander, I said, 'I thought you said Philip was a lovely geezer and would make a good husband for your daughter. So what's the odds if his ol' man *is* black?' That did it: my old man went absolutely berserk, almost as if he felt he'd been tricked into the visit and taking free booze. 'Shut your trap, you,' he said, looking at me menacingly with his ice-cold eyes. 'I've said that's the end of it, and I don't want to hear nuffink more abaht it.' And, sadly, that was that and nothing more was said on the subject. My big sister cried her eyes out and eventually married someone else on the rebound. That marriage didn't work, nor did the second, nor the third. My old Dad's bigoted thinking had a lot to answer for in my big sister's future!

Suffice to say, the journey to Uxbridge was uneventful. Let's face it, there ain't too much going to happen on the Piccadilly line is there? I came out of the station and followed the directions to the RAF station at Uxbridge, about a ten-minute walk away. The main contrast at Uxbridge to our square-bashing station was the living quarters. No Nissen huts here – just new and imposing five-storey blocks, with all mod cons including central heating! I believe the RAF band were housed in one of these blocks.

I did about a week's drill with the Advanced Drill Unit before our sergeant informed me that I was scheduled for a trial with the Bomber Command football team. Being young and supremely confident of my

'Eyes right!' *(RAF Museum, Hendon)*

own ability, I had no doubt that I would make the team. How wrong can you be with no experience of life? Only many years later, and with the benefit of hindsight, could I fully comprehend the enormity of my trial with the team. Household names from the world of football, whether English, Scottish, Welsh or Irish, had been sent to Uxbridge. And every man Jack of them was looking for that elusive cushy number in the haven of the sports store. And yet, little ol' me, a sometime reserve team player with Leyton Orient and presently on loan as a part-time pro in the Southern League, honestly, if naively, believed that he could make the team ahead of the big boys! I must confess that I got a big shock when I turned up for the trial. The present incumbent of my position of centre-forward, and the guy who actually ran the show, was none other than Eddie Firmani, a famous South African guy who was a member of Charlton Athletic and had recently played for England. The other forwards were all well-known Jocks from Glasgow Rangers and Celtic, while the rest of the Bomber Command team read like a who's who from the football league. There were a couple of guys from Arsenal and Chelsea and Spurs, then from Bolton Wanderers, Preston North End, Liverpool and Everton. Their names and their clubs just went on and on. But I soldiered on in the trial and didn't play too badly, with a few deft touches and a couple of shots on goal, before I was substituted for a Scottish international. Again, I was just a lad playing against seasoned pros, and to be perfectly honest they were on a different level to me. In fact, the whole squad played like I dreamed I could play!

So, Plan A hadn't worked: I hadn't made the team and now I was well and truly lumbered with the bullshit of the ADU. There were some plusses, though. If you weren't on guard duty, or the ADU didn't have a show to perform somewhere in the country, you got regular weekend passes. I recall vividly one week we were shipped up to Rhyl in North Wales because Her Majesty the Queen was going to visit the town. I must confess I thoroughly enjoyed the experience. I remember we lined the streets as she went past in her limo. We smartly presented arms in unison, and the crowds lining the streets all cheered heartily. Suddenly, this yobbo from up the Cally was enjoying being a player in the almost carnival-like atmosphere of a royal visit. If any of my old mates had seen me, I'd never have lived it down! But it was all too good to last. I had failed the football trial and I was way behind most of my flight in advanced drill

'If he speaks to you, keep looking straight ahead, and don't bloody look him in the eye. Understand?' 'Yes, Corporal.' *(RAF Museum, Hendon)*

performance. The RAF internal Mafia almost certainly had me on their list as a reject. All they needed was for me to supply them with a reasonable excuse to get shot of me. And I did just that!

Our drill sergeant had probably been primed to make me bite and lose my cool. One day we were doing our complicated drill with no commands, as we did on most days. I enjoyed this, and I thought I was pretty good at it. Suddenly, after we were told to stand at ease and for no apparent reason, the drill sergeant approached me and yelled for all the world to hear: 'Yew are a really ugly person, laddie,' he said, almost sticking his pace-stick up my nose. 'You've got a bloody awful posture,' he went on wickedly, 'and your chin is far too big to be on any ceremonial parades. What do you say to that, laddie?' Now this guy was no oil-painting himself. He had yellow teeth and BO. I thought to myself, I know he's digging me out for a reaction, but I ain't standing for that crap in front of all my mates. I stepped two paces forward and shouted out loudly, 'Permission to speak, Drill Sergeant?' He nodded his consent with

The air marshal is thanked by the station commander before flying home.
(RAF Museum, Hendon)

'Very smart, sergeant, very smart. Tell me, how long have you been here?' *(RAF Museum, Hendon)*

a knowing smirk on his face, looking around and smiling at the rest of the flight, who waited in eager anticipation for my reply. 'I may have a big chin, sir, but, with the greatest respect, the Drill Sergeant has got an even bigger mouth,' I shouted. 'And, if he would like to meet me back in the gym I will proceed to shut that big mouth and remove some of his yellow molars in the process.' I knew straightaway that I had sealed my own fate at Uxbridge. But it was worth it to hear the chuckles from the rest of the flight and to see the look of utter amazement on the drill sergeant's ugly boat race. He was the King at Uxbridge and nobody, but nobody, had ever spoken to him like that before. He was trembling with rage and going bright red in the face. It looked like he might be having a seizure! But, worst of all, he had lost face in front of the flight. He took a deep breath, composed himself, and marched towards me menacingly. 'H'according to Queen's Regulations,' he snarled, 'yew 'ave committed an offence by threatening a non-commissioned h'officer with violence. So,' he went on, 'I am a-putting you on a charge. Do you h'understand wot I am a-saying?' 'Yes, Drill Sergeant,' I shouted back in true RAF style. And, rather cheekily, I enquired, 'Does that mean the Drill Sergeant has declined my offer back at the gym?' What the hell, I thought. I'd been put on a 'fizzer', as we called it in the RAF, so I'll get my pound of flesh by taunting him on his shrine, the parade ground. Unusually for him, he couldn't wait to dismiss the flight, knowing full well that our differences of opinion would be all over the station by the same night. For sure, he'd certainly won the battle, but I had won the war! And I was quite satisfied, even if I had got nicked for my cheek!

A couple of days later, I was quick-marched into the squadron leader's office by a couple of huge military policemen, or SPs, as we called them in the RAF. For obvious reasons, I had never met our squadron leader before. I was surprised to see that he was so small that his chair seemed to totally envelop his tiny frame. The only big thing about him was his moustache, a real handlebar job on his top lip. He ordered me to stand at ease and started looking at some papers on his desk. Then, in a thin reedy voice, he said almost wearily, 'Now look here, laddie, this is just not on. You can't go around the place threatening my NCOs with violence, what what? So what have you got to say for yourself before I pass sentence?' What a bloody sham, I thought to myself. I've been neatly fitted up and he already knows what he's going to do with me before I even open my mouth. 'Permission to speak sir?' I yelled out. He jumped at the sound of my loud voice and, waving his right arm airily, said, 'Yes, yes, get on with it lad, for God's sake.' 'The Drill Sergeant has made a mistake, sir,' I said. 'He offered me a challenge and I only responded, sir.' He bent down over his desk again, fussing over his pile of papers and looking as though he was getting thoroughly cheesed off with the whole business. He took a deep breath and said fussily, 'No, no laddie, this is just not on, simply because the evidence totally contradicts your statement.' Then he went into his regular spiel for the airmen who were on his reject list – God only knows how many times he'd said it! 'Here on the Advanced Drill Unit,' he said, 'we never implement any of the charges. What we prefer to do is ship nasty people like you away from Uxbridge to a punishment posting, do you understand, laddie?' That was more or less what I'd expected, but it beat doing time in the Glasshouse. So I replied by saying, 'Yes, sir,

I understand. Thank you very much, sir.' And that was just about that. The squadron leader handed me my new posting, already neatly made out, of course, as I'd had no chance in hell of being found not guilty! I looked down casually at the travel warrant, which read, 'RAF Bassingbourn'. I politely enquired where the devil was RAF Bassingbourn, and even he didn't have a clue. So I was marched out and yet another reject had been sent on his way! In fact, nobody at Uxbridge had the vaguest idea as to the whereabouts of RAF Bassingbourn. The general consensus of opinion was that if it was a punishment posting, it was very likely to be up in the Highlands of Scotland, or some other God-forsaken place!

This guessing game went on for days, until it was finally time to say goodbye to all my mates in the ADU and spend another week at home. The RAF 'Bush Telegraph' was a very powerful weapon in the days of national service – and probably is to this very day. My unfair reputation as a nutter who wanted to whack drill sergeants had probably reached my new posting even before I had, and no doubt the local hard men would be waiting to sort me out! I was quite happy to leave Uxbridge, as all that bullshit wasn't really my cup of tea. I had gone there for one specific purpose, and that had failed.

WHERE'S BASSINGBOURN?

So, it was back home on the Piccadilly line for the last time during my national service. Another boozy week's leave and lots of womanising. We all came out of a pub one night, well sloshed and feeling a bit randy. 'Del Boy' Jones, one of my closest mates and the best man at my wedding, happened to say, 'I've worked it out: by the time you've chatted up a bird, took her out for a drink and a meal, then got a slap for taking liberties, you might just as well go down West and spend the same sort of money on a brass and get what you've paid for.' The other guys nodded in agreement. I thought about what he said and it made sense. What sort of nice young girl would do us boozy yobs a favour? We all piled into a 'lobster and crab' (cab) and paid the cabbie off in Wardour Street. Suddenly, the others went all funny – even Del Boy, who had made the original suggestion, bottled out. But not me. I went steaming in like a stallion to a big busty lady standing on the corner. 'D'ya want business, luv?' she enquired, still puffing on her fag. I could see all the guys watching me, so I just nodded without even asking the price. I didn't have a clue about the going rate anyway! She led me down an alley just off Wardour Street, took my dough, leant against the wall while still puffing away on her fag, and started fumbling, with me trying to put the condom on. I was young and inexperienced – a virgin, in fact – and I'd never had a 'knee-trembler' before. Actually I'd never had much of anything before and I was beginning to quite enjoy the experience. All at once, a torch was shone in my face and a loud voice boomed out, ''Allo 'allo, what's going on 'ere?' I couldn't mistake the outline of the helmet, it was the ol' bill and he had me bang to rights committing an illegal act. So, ever the clever Dick – no pun intended – I tried to talk my way out of it. 'I beg your pardon, officer,' I said in my poshest voice, while adjusting my clothes, 'I've just brought my girlfriend down here for a goodnight kiss.' The huge copper stuck his stubbly chin almost onto my nose and enquired in an almost fatherly manner, 'Is that so, smart-arse? If she's your bleedin' girlfriend, why is it I've moved her out of here four times tonight, wiv four different geezers? Now piss off before I nick ya.'

That was my very first and my very last experience with a brass. I limped gingerly away with a Groucho Marx-type walk, with the lads curled up with laughter and the condom still pulling painfully on my now shrunken manhood! Yet again I had done my hard-earned dosh in cold blood! But strange to say, my actions in Wardour Street had earned me some bonus points in the eyes of my mates. Even my two best muckers, Del Boy Jones and Lenny Cairns, were impressed. The three of us had grown up together after the war up the Cally, and I remember the giggles we'd had when we joined the Boy Scouts.

Now we were young yobbos and not the least bit interested in Lord Baden-Powell and his dream of converting deprived British lads into decent citizens worthy of dying for their King and Country! We weren't remotely inspired by woodcraft or learning to tie soppy knots with a rope, even though success in such activities meant an extra badge to sew onto your brown shirt. The 27th North London troop was a shambles. However, we did enjoy all the football and the weekend camps at places like Gilwell Park and Ashdown Forest, where we could chat up the Girl Guides, stare at their boobs and sit around the blazing fire at night-time singing strange songs like, 'Ging gang gooli, gooli-gooli, watcha, ging gang goo, ging gang goo'. I never had a clue what the song meant, and more than sixty years on I still don't! Being an old thespian at heart, I really enjoyed dressing up for the annual gang show made popular later on by the Canadian guy Ralph Reader, who turned the gang shows into national events. All the mums and dads turned up on the big night, and it evoked really good vibes to light up my drab teenage years.

But the practice of using the scouting facilities just for our own means was about to end. A new scoutmaster had arrived on the scene and wasn't like the old boy before him, who had let us do more or less what we pleased. I can still remember the new guy's name – Bert Kerley. He was muscular, with a diamond-shaped face and some sparse, crinkly ginger hair on his nut. He worked on the *Daily Mirror*, was a tasty footballer, and played regularly in one of the senior Sunday leagues. Unfortunately for us, he was also a 'Holy Joe' and a stickler for the Boy Scout Rules. In his eyes this meant going to church every Sunday, to our parish church St Andrew's in Thornhill Square. That wasn't the end of our penance: we also had to visit the vicarage once a week for Bible classes and listen to the mad old vicar rambling on about some rubbish. Bert gave our gang an ultimatum because he had tumbled us. No church and no Bible classes on a regular basis, then you'd be drummed out of the troop. Most of the guys left immediately, but I stuck it out because I enjoyed the sporting activities. My actions were misinterpreted by Bert, who wrongly believed I had also got a call from Jesus. So, I had it away a bit lively!

I must digress a while to paint a picture of my two best mates, whom I had knocked around with since junior school. Del Boy Jones's garden in Belitha Villas was opposite our Nan's garden in Offord Road, and we moved in with her after the war ended. I remember Del with much affection, and I still see him when we're invited down to his grand estate in Essex. More about his grand estate later! Del Boy was completely fearless, an absolute nutter, and would never bottle out of anything. He took up boxing at an early age and we all used to go and watch him at the shows in all the local town halls. Now, Del couldn't box to save his life, but he couldn't half fight! I remember one evening when he was drawn against this big, muscular black guy and the guy beat the shit out of Del. But still Del wouldn't give in, even though his face was covered in 'claret'! Another time, so I was told, Del bumped into a local gang on his way out from the Cally Baths. This vicious little firm was four-handed, but Del stood up to all of them and got a terrible hiding. Del's old man was a whisky-swilling, ex-prison warder – just like my old man, even down to the drink. I was round Del's house one day and we were messing around with his Dad's handcuffs. To cut a long story short, I persuaded Del to put them on – he would do just about anything for a dare. Then I promptly ran back to my house with the keys, leaving Del to eat his dinner in the cuffs! Funny, that – his ol' man never took kindly to me after that incident and his old Mum had the hump with me as well for many years.

While we were all away doing our national service, Del Boy, who had failed his medical because of dodgy eardrums, got matey with the younger brother of one of the local villains. All at once, the two of them had opened a flash nightclub in Islington – I can only surmise where all the readies came from! I went up to their club a few times, but it wasn't really my scene because it had become the haunt for all the local villains – and some not so local. They were all there with their firms. The Diamond Boys from the Angel; the Flanagan twins from up the Cally; the Nashes from Hoxton; and sometimes even Ronnie, Reggie and Charlie Kray. I can still picture Del Boy strutting around in his immaculate tuxedo, chatting to all the birds – and he did love the ladies! I suppose with his blond hair and dimpled chin he could have passed as a young Alan Ladd, but only if you had dodgy 'minces'! I heard on the grapevine that the club was losing money and then I read in the local paper that it had mysteriously burned down! The insurance money must have helped Del and his partner to open a betting shop in Dalston soon after the fire. They sold that to one of the big companies after a couple of years, and the next news I had of Del was that he had a lovely house in Hertfordshire and was flogging second-hand cars down Warren Street. Later, I got the news that Del had bought a farm in deepest Essex and that he was breeding horses, out riding with the local hunt and the point-to-point races and mixing with the country set. The local boy from up the Cally had done good and how he had obtained his dosh is not really any of my business! Del and his lovely wife Jean, who incidentally was part of our gang for many years and was a good mate of mine, decided to turn their farm into a doggery and a cattery – a nice, cosy place where the well-off could leave their pets safely when they went away, and a nice little earner. Sadly, one evening Jean went inside the house to make some tea while Del locked the animals up for the night and when Del came back into the kitchen, he found her lying dead on the floor from a massive heart attack. Sadly, I only found out about this tragedy a couple of years later because Del was far too shocked and distraught to do anything or tell anybody. However, after years of being depressed, happily Del Boy has bounced back again and now he's letting his two sons run the business while he visits the fleshpots of the French Riviera with his new lady.

My other best mate was Lenny Cairns. Lenny and his lovely wife Margaret were killed in a terrible road accident near Cape Town in South Africa. Lenny lived close to me when our family eventually moved to Twyford Street, and we were inseparable. He was dark and handsome with flashing brown eyes, and a very snappy dresser. The girls loved Lenny and in fact I got all of his leftovers! Lenny became a London cabbie the year before I passed the 'Knowledge'. Like my family, all his uncles worked down the old Covent Garden Market. Our drinking den, also that of Lenny's uncles, was the Sutton Arms on the corner of Copenhagen Street and the Cally. One day a new guv'nor arrived with his wife and charming daughter Margaret to take over the pub. This new boss was a lovely man called John. He had been a POW of the Japs and had toiled on the notorious Burma Railroad with great suffering. He couldn't possibly get away with it today, but would you believe, he flatly refused to serve anyone who looked remotely Japanese! I was the first to ask Margaret out, but what we had was only platonic. Then Lenny started taking her out and eventually they got married and had a couple of lovely sons, one now a London cabbie himself. Lenny, like me, worked out at Heathrow Airport, and he got friendly with this guy who owned a chain of luxury hotels back at his home in South Africa. The friendship continued to blossom over the years, and Margaret and Lenny were invited over to South Africa for a marvellous holiday with their wealthy friends. The guy really took a shine to Lenny's quick cockney wit and charming manner, so he asked him if the family would like to move to South Africa, with Lenny working for him at one of his plush hotels as a 'greeter'. His job would be to drive to the airport to meet and greet any important clients.

So, after a long delay in selling their house, one fine summer's day the Cairns family packed their cases in Palmers Green for the very last time and headed out for a new life in South Africa. Round about Christmas time, Lenny invited his mate and his wife over for a holiday. They decided to hire a car and take a tour around the Cape. Lenny did the first stint of driving, then his mate took over with Margaret and Lenny resting in the back – not wearing seatbelts, I might add. Suddenly, an old tatty bus came roaring towards them on the dirt road. The driver lost control on the loose gravel and the bus veered towards their car and hit it sideways on. Lenny and his wife were thrown out and killed. It's very strange what fate hands out, isn't it? Who knows – if Lenny had managed to sell his house without such a long delay, the fatal scenario could well have been altered. What a terrible waste of two lovely people!

But back to my new posting. I couldn't even be bothered to look at the map and find out where the hell my next camp was situated. Why worry? I thought. Even if RAF Bassingbourn happened to be in 'High Street, China', I'd still have to go there and do the rest of my time, whether I liked it or not!

The usual chain of events occurred once my leave had finished: say goodbye to everyone, get all my kit together and go striding down the familiar Caledonian Road to King's Cross. Just leaving from King's Cross station had to be a clue to my destination, I thought to myself as I marched down the road. In those far-off days, King's Cross was the old LNER, the London North-Eastern Railway, and it hugged the east coast right up to Scotland. I chuckled at the predicament I had got myself into by being Jack the Lad and letting my mouth take over my brain. If I had said nowt and took it on the chin, I might have lasted the distance at Uxbridge and still be enjoying those weekend passes. But no, not me. My big mouth had got me into trouble yet again, and now I was heading for a posting that no living soul seemed to know about. But at least the guy who made out the travel warrant must have known where I was going – I hope he did, anyway! However, surprise surprise, it appeared my guardian angel had been watching over me. I approached the ticket office and handed over my travel warrant to the guy behind the desk. He looked closely at the destination and said in a bored voice the magic words, 'You're in the wrong place, mate, you need the Suburban line for Bassingbourn. But you'll 'ave to change at Potters Bar 'cos they are working on the track.' How strange to relate my experiences of over fifty years ago and mention Potters Bar and 'track repairs' – it was only a short time ago that passengers were tragically killed at the very same station, possibly because of faulty track repairs.

I wandered round to the Suburban platform, still totally unaware of the whereabouts of RAF Bassingbourn, and handed my travel warrant to the ticket-collector. 'Change at Potters Bar 'cos of track repairs,' he said, 'then take a train to Royston.' 'So where's Royston, mate?' I asked. 'And where the 'ell is Bassingbourn?' He gave me a funny look as though he thought I was taking the mickey out of him, then said mockingly, 'You mean to tell me you've got a travel warrant to a place and you don't know where the bloody place is?' He chuckled to himself at his own humour, and then said laughingly, 'I do 'ope you can find your way around a bit better when you're up in your bleedin' airplane.' 'Listen, mate,' I said wearily, 'I'm not taking the mickey, please can you tell me where Bassingbourn is located, 'cos I ain't got a clue.' He reached down into his little drawer, pulled out a map and, sticking his finger onto a page, he said, with feeling, 'This 'ere is Royston, mate, which is on the very borders of Hertfordshire and Cambridgeshire.' Then, moving his finger an inch or so to the right, he said, 'And this 'ere is Bassingbourn, about a ten-minute bus ride away towards Cambridge, got it?'

I thanked him for his help and walked onto the platform in a state of some excitement. Who knows, I thought, maybe I've walked away from a pile of dung and fallen into a heap of diamonds. My new posting was near enough for me to get home, just as long as I could talk my way into some weekend passes! This punishment posting was starting to look like it might well turn out to be just the opposite. My mind was racing away during the short journey, first to Potters Bar then on to Royston. What was the camp like? Was there any bull? Could I get myself a cushy number and be able to slide off every weekend to play soccer and earn some dough? I wouldn't have to wait long for the answers! I got on the local bus which made its way along a narrow, country road – well, not much more than a lane really – then through a pretty little village with a sign that read 'Bassingbourn'.

I need to pause for a minute to tell you an amusing story that happened to me nearly half a century after my first glimpse of my new surroundings in Bassingbourn. I've been a London cabbie for some four decades, and last year I picked up a young American couple at Heathrow Airport. They weren't too sure of their destination, but they knew it was in the general direction of Cambridge. We agreed a fair price and off we went. I saw them studying a map intently as I looked through the driving mirror and, being a helpful person, I turned on the intercom and asked if I could be of any assistance. 'Yeah, we gotta problem, cabbie,' the guy drawled. 'We know the name of the goddam place, but we can't for the hell of it find it on the map.' 'So, what's the name of the place?' I enquired casually. Why I thought I should know any more than they did about the location of a small English village in the heart of the country, I don't know. But that's the way I am! The Yank placed his finger on the map and uttered those 'immortal' words that would make me a star. 'I guess you would pronounce it Bass-ing-bourn,' he said. 'But it's one helluva name.' My moment of fame and adoration has arrived, I thought. Now I can claim my moment of glory. So I said, almost patronisingly, 'Can you find Royston, which is on the very borders of Hertfordshire?' He moved his index finger across the map and found it straightaway, because Royston is a major market town. He nodded his head in excitement, and I continued, 'If you move your finger eastward on the road to Cambridge, you should find what you are looking for.' I carried on watching them through the driving mirror as he traced his finger along the map. 'Gee whizz!' he suddenly yelled. 'I've just found the goddam place!' Turning to his wife, he said, 'I know these cabbie guys are hot in London, but this guy knows the whole damn country.' Now was the perfect time to sell myself just in case I could chat them into a future lucrative tour of places like Stonehenge, Windsor or the like! 'Oh yes,' I said, telling a 'porkie', 'I specialise in tours all over the country. So if you ever want a tour, I'm your man.' They were suitably impressed by my fantastic knowledge of the 'whole' of England, and rewarded me generously when we got to our destination.

But what a change to the whole area from half a century ago. We used to stand in two old sentry boxes in the lane and when the phone rang, to indicate an aircraft coming in to land, we used to run outside with our red flags and stop the traffic! It's hard to believe, but, cross my heart, it's the truth. This lane was now a major road, bordered by many ugly housing estates. The village pub, where me and my mates had spent many a happy hour, was now gone. And, amazingly, the whole area around the old runway was now a golf course, would you believe! Within fifty years, the whole landscape had turned from countryside to commuter-land. It's very sad and very frightening to think what we are doing to our heritage. Will England become a concrete jungle in a generation's time? If we don't take a sensible step backwards and try to comprehend what we are destroying, future generations will curse us for our short-sightedness! Unfortunately, even though I gave them one of my business cards, I never heard from the American couple again. So if this book ever gets read by that particular couple, may I offer my sincere apologies for appearing to be such a smart-arse and attempting to gain some financial reward under false pretences! But hey, what the hell. How many of the estimated 24,000 London cabbies would have known the whereabouts of a tiny village like little ol' Bassingbourn anyway?

But I digress – back to fifty years ago. The old bus pulled up outside the camp and the driver shouted out laughingly, using his well-worn, standard funny joke, 'All RAF personnel, get ready to bale out!' I gathered my kit together, stepped off the bus, and stopped to survey my new home for the next couple of years – if I could keep my nose clean. The entrance to the camp was much like any other RAF establishment. But what caught my eye were the three capital letters after the name: 'OCU'. I was intrigued – what was an OCU? I showed my papers to the guy on the gate and asked the burning question, 'What does the OCU stand for, mate?' 'That means Operational Conversion Unit,' he replied in a friendly way. Then, seeing the look of complete ignorance on my face, he went on knowingly, 'Let me explain, mate. After the young officers get their wings, they come here and learn how to fly Canberra bombers.' He paused to have a sly drag on his ciggie and, looking over his shoulder, he whispered, 'It's a piece of cake 'ere, mate, 'cos they have day and night flying and nobody bothers you.' 'So there ain't any bull?' I enquired. 'Course not, you dummy,' he said. 'The guys on nights are all kipping in the day and vice versa for the day shift. All the Groupie is concerned abaht is keeping his effing planes flying for twenty-four bleedin' hours a day.' He took another quick look behind, then said with a big grin on his face, 'You need to find yourself a nice quiet little number and you'll disappear from view.' He then muttered, 'Keep your nose clean and stay well clear of the Chief Warrant Officer, he's an arse-hole. And,' he said, as I thanked him, 'if you want any dodgy American snout, I'm your man.'

This punishment posting of mine could well turn out to be a bonus, I thought to myself. If there's day and night flying, it stands to reason that there won't be any bull. And if I keep my nose clean and lick a few important boots, who knows, I might be creeping off home every weekend

A lot of the station staff had seen active service in the war. You only had to look at the gongs they were wearing – DSOs, DFCs and the like – to appreciate they'd got some time in and been shot at, too. *(RAF Museum, Hendon)*

to play footie! My lesson in life had been learned the hard way. Keep your big mouth shut and always be subservient to officers and NCOs, with plenty of 'Yes, sirs' and 'No, sirs'. In effect, adopt the practice described by the very popular American colloquialism 'kissing arse'. After getting directions to my quarters from the guy on the gate, I ambled into RAF Bassingbourn and started taking in some of the scenery. Most of the guys were dressed in filthy grease-stained overalls in a sort of dirty green colour. And many of them looked as though they needed a bloody good bath and a shave, not forgetting the regulation haircut! They gave me some funny looks as they passed by, and why not? I was wearing my peaked 'postman's hat' and my boots were gleaming in the midday sun, while my best blues were neatly pressed and in pristine Uxbridge condition. I looked so smart compared to that rabble, it was almost embarrassing!

I eventually found my quarters after a few near misses and threw my gear down on an empty bed, chuckling away to myself as I looked around at what would be my home for the next couple of years. Compared to my immaculate quarters at Uxbridge, the place was an absolute tip. True, the beds had been made in a fashion, but they would have been torn asunder by the inspecting NCOs at Uxbridge. And the same NCOs would have gone absolutely berserk if they had seen the state of some of the lockers by the beds. It looked as though the entire contents had been literally thrown in from a great height, then the doors had been forced half-shut to stop the whole lot from falling out again! The ancient and decrepit table in the middle of the hut was almost groaning under the weight of the piles of old newspapers and magazines stacked on top of it. I wandered across to check out my new comrades' reading habits and couldn't help but snigger at what I found. Flicking through the explicit mags, I smiled again at the thought of sharing quarters with a bunch of perverts and sex maniacs!

'Present arms!' *(RAF Museum, Hendon)*

These mags really were something else, certainly never seen in my last camp.

My mental inspection of the quarters was broken by a good old cockney voice saying loudly, 'Can I 'elp you, mate?' I looked across the room and there, sitting up in bed, was this tiny little figure of a guy in pyjamas. I thought to myself that this little fella must be nicknamed 'Tiny', 'Nipper' or even 'Shorty', and I was bang on: I found out later that he was indeed nicknamed 'Half-Pint'. 'You alright, mate?' I replied. 'I've been a bad boy and been posted 'ere from Uxbridge.' He smiled, leaned across to light a ciggie, and said with a wicked grin on his face, 'Not anuvver geezer with a punishment posting? This camp is banged out with bad boys from just about every RAF station in the UK. So what did you do?' he continued, joking. 'Was you caught screwing the CO's missus behind the officers' married quarters?' 'Naw,' I replied, 'nuffing as exciting as that. They reckon I threatened to duff up an arse-hole of a drill sergeant.' 'If he was an arse-hole,' he said, puffing away, 'I reckon you're entitled to give 'im a dig. Some of those bastards fink they are bleedin' Adolf, bleedin' 'itler, now they've got two or three effing stripes on their arm.'

I liked this little fella right from the off. He was one of my own, as we cockneys say. A Bermondsey boy who stuck to me like shite on a blanket for the rest of our service. I had the front, the chat and the muscle, and Half-Pint had the cunning of a predator and the bottle to slice someone with a 'chiv' (razor). Many years later while enjoying the gangster movies from Hollywood, I thought the actors Danny Devito and Joe Pesci were dead ringers for Half-Pint. Small in stature, but frighteningly vicious in a punch-up! 'So,' I enquired, 'why ain't you working?' 'I ain't working,' he said, puffing away on his ciggie like a man possessed, 'because I've been bleedin' up all night, bleedin' freezing my cods off on effing guard duty. But why they ever bovver 'aving bleedin' effing guards protecting this piss-'ole, I'll never know. There ain't nuffink 'ere worth nicking. I mean, who the eff wants to buy an effing Canberra jet?' I chuckled at his coarse humour, then walked across to his bed, shook his hand, and introduced myself. He smiled up at me, still puffing away on his ciggie, and said with a big grin on his face, 'You'd better get shot of that pouffie uniform, Alf, before the boys get back, or they'll forever be taking the piss.'

All the guys starting coming in and flopping down on their bunks, shouting out, 'Stuff the bleedin' RAF and their thirty bob a week for effing manual labour.' After being introduced to all the guys by Half-Pint, I suddenly began to realise that this motley crew, myself now included, were the RAF's 'Mrs Mopps'. None of them had the slightest interest in the RAF and none of them had the remotest inclination whatsoever to better themselves by studying for a trade during their service. They were quite happy to spend their time ducking and diving and skiving, polishing a few floors and emptying a few ashtrays – but keeping their noses clean in the process. My grandiose plans of settling down in luxury as an assistant PTI in a sports store had gone awry in a big way. Now I had lumbered myself with a bunch of no-hopers and the future didn't look too rosy. Again, how wrong can first impressions be? They turned out to be a great bunch of guys and had their so-called duties well and truly sewn up. They knew every trick in the book and some more besides to get off cookhouse duties and any other chores, and in me they had found a willing student. I swear to God that some of the old hands could even read what the NCOs were thinking, even before they gave us the orders. Consequently, they laid their plans in advance to thwart the order. Let me give you an example further down the line. One of the guys had heard on the grapevine that some chemical was on the way to kill the stubborn weeds on the runway. Now, everyone knew that we would be the firm to spread the dangerous stuff. So one of the studious guys in the gang – they called him 'Brains' because he always had his nose in a book – checked out Queen's Regulations to read up on the safety precautions when handling 'toxic and volatile substances'. Anyway, to cut a long story sideways, when we were ordered to spread this stuff on the runway, Brains started giving the young NCO a real earbashing. 'According to Queen's Regulations,' said Brains, 'any such person who gives the order without first having made doubly sure his men have been adequately protected against any toxic substances is liable to court martial should any of the said men suffer as a consequence of that said order.' The young NCO quickly bottled out and we never even reached the runway!

What I admired about my fellow Mrs Mopps was their constant ability to work as a team against the RAF establishment. If one of the team was threatened with a charge by a bolshie, young NCO, then our 'negotiator' – if it was the Mafia, he would probably be known as the 'consigliere' – would pay him a call and tell him ever so politely over a friendly pint that if he decided to proceed with the charge, then he would have to suffer a

One for the album, outside the billet. *(RAF Museum, Hendon)*

constant policy of non-cooperation from every man on the team. No, no, not mutiny; this firm was too cute to mention that. This policy of non-cooperation could consist of a deliberate go-slow, with the loss of his valuable drinking time, or even regular formal complaints to the CO, backed up by all the lads of course, accusing the NCO of bullying or even sexual harassment! It doesn't matter what rank you reach in the services – all anyone is looking for is a quiet life. And the very last thing you need is bolshie airmen constantly telling porkies to the CO, resulting in your being dragged up before him every week to answer a string of false allegations. Most of the young NCOs invariably bottled out and took the easy option, just for a quiet life! The one exception, way down the line, was a tough little 'Jock' from the Gorbals in Glasgow. I'll give the guy his due, he didn't give a toss about our threats and offered us outside one at a time, or two at a time, if we fancied our chances! We needed to get him off our patch, but how could the team manage it? Well, like many other Jocks he had an Achilles' heel – he couldn't keep off the hard stuff. So we enlisted the help of a 'face' outside our team – not for nothing, mind you. And he just happened to be in the village pub when our Jock came in. They struck up a friendship, with our man plying him with drinks, and before long he was absolutely legless. Then an 'argument' ensued, someone just happened to call the ol' bill, and he was nicked for being drunk and disorderly. We never saw the Jock corporal again! Some liberal-minded persons may argue that our modus operandi was grossly unfair, but more of those tales later. I reckoned that by sheer good fortune and a large slice of luck, I had found probably the cushiest number anywhere in the RAF!

CHAPTER FOUR

Doing My Time at RAF Bassingbourn

Right from the off, I found my new posting absolutely fascinating. It really was a totally different world. I had come from a camp that viewed bullshit almost as a religion and shorn heads, gleaming boots and uniforms pressed to precision with razor-sharp creases had been considered par for the course! I remember the times when as we walked around Uxbridge, we were forever saluting officers and being harangued by drill sergeants shouting out things like, 'Come over 'ere you 'orrible little man!' Then, I'd have to walk over, stand to attention, and listen to this moron spout out his normal diatribe. 'Are you feeling any pain, laddie?' they would scream in your ear. 'No, Drill Sergeant!' you would yell back in age-old fashion. 'Well you should be, you 'orrible little man, 'cos I'm standing on your bloody hair, so get it cut ASAP, alright?' they'd scream. 'Yes, Drill Sergeant!' you'd yell in reply. Then a smart about-turn and march off, muttering to myself under my breath, 'You are a bunch of wankers, Drill Sergeants, and I hate every one of you stupid bastards.'

The Uxbridge drill sergeants would have gone apoplectic if they could have seen the absolute 'shower' that inhabited my present home. To say that the hairstyles were long is an understatement. They were almost beatnik in length, very often tied back in a mini ponytail! The berets and uniforms weren't even RAF blue any more, more of a dirty grey from the constant grease and dirt from the planes. And as for the boots, they made me curl up in fits of laughter. Not a semblance of any polish whatsoever and more akin to trekking or mountaineering boots, heavily coated in grease! But it was the laid-back attitude of all the ground crews that really amazed me. For obvious reasons, there was a strong rapport between them and the commissioned officers in the air crews. The air crews relied on them for their very existence and who knows, if they had started to pull rank on them the planes may not have been quite as safe and secure as they might have been! First thing in the morning you would often see the ground crews and air crews walking across to the canteens for their breakfast after having been working and flying all night. The ground crews' uniforms all looked as though their owners had been diving in barrels of oil and the young pilots didn't look much better, wearing tatty old scarves that may well have been lucky omens but they wouldn't have seemed out of place in a charity shop! Not a single member of either crew would be wearing the regulation RAF beret, and they'd all be laughing and puffing on ciggies as they made their way to their different canteens.

So, the whole practice of saluting officers really went out of the window at Bassingbourn. If they were all wearing their flying gear on duty, you might well be saluting a technician checking out the plane! In fact, the same sort of experience happened to me further down the line. A couple of my mates worked in the stores where the air crews collected their flying gear. I chatted up a couple of the young pilots for a ride in a plane. Not a big Canberra jet bomber, though – no way! They told me to turn up at the stores early the next day, when they would be flying an Anson up to

Bassingbourn from the air.
(RAF Museum, Hendon)

Blenheim light bombers of the RAF's 104 Squadron were among the first residents at Bassingbourn in 1939.
(RAF Museum, Hendon)

Doncaster. Suddenly it didn't seem a good idea any more, and I was so nervous I thought I might have to wear bicycle clips to cover any subsequent embarrassment! Nevertheless, I was at the stores bright and early the following morning, but still feeling apprehensive 'cos I had never flown before. Let's face it, there ain't much opportunity of a plane ride up the Caledonian Road, is there? My mate kitted me out in the full regalia of the flying suit, plus a bleedin' great parachute, and I followed the pilots on board. I sat down gingerly on a hard wooden seat behind them. The doors were shut with a bang, and then all at once, with an almighty noise that frightened the life out of me, the engines roared into life. There was a lot of bumping, rattling and squeaking, and suddenly we were up in the air and I was a genuine airman at last.

Strangely, I quite enjoyed the trip and loved looking down on the beautiful English countryside. However, after about half an hour we began to curl over at right angles and the beautiful English countryside was starting to look a bit iffy and a funny shape! We started to lose height rapidly, the ground seemed to be rushing up, and I wished to God that I had worn those bicycle clips! All the bumping, rattling and squeaking started again as we hit the deck and taxied to a hangar. I knew immediately from that day that I wasn't cut out to be a real flyer, or even a sailor for that matter! For sure, I still fly once a year to play my beloved golf in Spain or Portugal, but I need to be 'Brahms and Liszt' just to get on board!

I recall we had to pick up some important boxes in Doncaster, so when the door was swung open I stepped outside to help. That's when all the young 'erks' started saluting me, wrongly believing that I was an officer. So I ran back inside the plane again, giggling like a big kid. The young pilots saw the funny side of it and had a good laugh at my expense. Our return journey was especially exciting, as the pilot let me sit in his seat while he went back and had a kip and his co-pilot took over the controls. It's God's honest truth, but by the time we landed at Bassingbourn my hands and feet were wet with nervous sweat! Yeah, a truly great experience, but never again – well, only to play golf.

You'll have to excuse me for all this digressing – I'm racing ahead of myself as the good memories keep flooding my brain! I duly reported to the flight lieutenant in charge of our flight on my arrival at Bassingbourn and was informed of my duties. This flight looie, who in effect was my

The Canberra was the RAF's first jet bomber. *(RAF Museum, Hendon)*

immediate guv'nor, was a really lovely, laid-back guy. He wasn't a career officer – in fact he was just like me, a national service man who had been selected from POM, potential officer material, a very rare occurrence for a national service guy. And, would you Adam-and-Eve it, he was a football nut. In fact, he was the only commissioned officer playing for the Bassingbourn team. I don't know if the RAF Mafia were still at it, but he certainly knew that I played pro soccer and he wanted me in his team. He didn't beat about the bush, telling me bluntly that if I wanted to earn money playing football at the weekend, then he would grant me my early chits provided that I played for his beloved Bassingbourn football team in their mid-week games. As they say in the Mafia movies, it was an offer I couldn't refuse!

As it happens, we became close mates – well, as close as an officer and an AC2 could become – and out of respect to his rank, I only called him Peter when we were alone. He often picked up me and my two mates in his little car every Thursday for away fixtures. We would stop for a couple of pints in the local hostelries while on our way to the many RAF Bomber Command stations all over East Anglia and beyond. These were famous RAF stations with names that conjured up epic bombing raids of the Second World War, for example Duxford, Coltishall, Lakenheath and many others – not forgetting Scampton, the home of 617 Squadron, the celebrated Dambusters. The story of the Dambusters has always fascinated me. Most people, including 'Bomber' Harris, the head of Bomber Command, thought that Barnes Wallis and his theory of the bouncing bomb were barmy. Not so the AOC, his superior, who reckoned the concept might well be effective against the two giant dams situated deep in Germany's industrial heartland. Heavy standard bombing had already proved ineffective against the two key dams, as they needed to be hit way down towards the bottom of their massive structures for maximum effect.

The Canberra first flew in 1949 and entered service with the RAF in 1951. *(RAF Museum, Hendon)*

The Yanks took over Bassingbourn from the RAF in 1942. *(RAF Museum, Hendon)*

Barnes Wallis and his team carried on testing his bomb – still not proven on any bombing raid. Top air crews were selected from every bomber squadron in the RAF and sent to Scampton with their Lancasters for a five-week training course. This consisted of low flying at night – and when they said low, they meant very low! The boffins had estimated that the Lancasters would have to attack at about 40ft to get the angle right for the bouncing bomb to do the job properly! And that wasn't the only worry for the pilots. The dams were heavily protected with sophisticated ack-ack batteries, and high cliffs had to be cleared at the completion of their bombing runs. The man put in command of 617 Squadron was the legendary Wing Commander Guy Gibson, and only three crews failed to pass the course and make the final raid. As all the world now knows, the bouncing bomb succeeded and the dams were destroyed. For sure, these stations will be forever etched in RAF history, and we played footie at all of them. One day when it was just the flight looie and me, we stopped off on the way back for tea and cakes at his house and he introduced me to his charming wife and two kids. I vaguely remember seeing Peter's name in the papers many years later, when he was presented with some sort of long-service medal. The RAF must have persuaded him to sign on again, because by then he had made squadron leader.

In all honesty, I didn't do too much during my time at Bassingbourn. I certainly didn't do any work in the day, but a team of us tidied some offices and buffed a few shiny floors after the occupants had finished at teatime. We'd go through the motions for a couple of hours, then creep off to the NAAFI for a few bevvies. No wonder they nicknamed us 'The Skiving Mob'! Most evenings we could be found in the village pub, telling all the local girls about our 'daredevil deeds' in the air. They weren't too impressed with our fairy stories, because the Yanks had been there long before us and they could tell a *good* fairy story! On top of that, they had plenty of readies to spend to back up all their claims. Be fair, how could you possibly impress nubile young ladies on our meagre wages of thirty bob a week – especially if you were big and ugly in the first place?

Again, this time through no fault of my own, I got into trouble, got charged and was confined to quarters for a month. That meant, in effect, no weekend passes and no footie money. All our boozy gang had been celebrating a birthday down at the local, and we returned to camp absolutely legless. One of our mates worked as a cook, so we all traipsed into the cookhouse late at night and he started making us fried egg sandwiches. To this day, I still don't know what really happened. I remember this huge brass tureen, full to the brim with boiling water or soup. And I remember the old black cat who was tucking into the bits of meat I had thrown onto the floor for him. Suddenly, I heard this agonising scream from the old moggy and the angry voice of someone shouting out, 'You stupid drunken bastard, you'll get us all effing nicked.' Then suddenly everyone was on their toes and running. I began to run as well as I could manage, even though I didn't have a drunken clue why I was running. It turned out that one of the guys, well full of booze, had been messing about with the old cat and had dropped it into the boiling water to a very sad and painful death. Even to this very day I still don't know who it was, or whether it was deliberate or just a drunken prank that went horribly wrong, all down to the demon drink.

Suffice to say, the whole gang of us were hauled up in front of the CO and given a right rollicking. This CO, a group captain, was a really nice old guy. He must have been near the end of his RAF career and this drunken display by some of his airmen was the very last thing he wanted on his record, especially if the local papers happened to pick it up. I remember noticing his thick grey hair as he bent over to read the charges.

The airfield had opened just before the war, but was still a bit rough around the edges when the Americans arrived with their Flying Fortresses. *(RAF Museum, Hendon)*

Flying Forts of the 91st Bomb Group flew daylight raids over Germany and like their RAF predecessors with their Blenheims suffered heavy losses, 197 in fact. This one's from the 322nd Bomb Squadron. *(RAF Museum, Hendon)*

He took in a deep breath, sighed, then looked up to us and said in an impeccable accent, 'Gentlemen, what the devil are we to do with you lot?' Looking down again at the charges, he said, 'I'm going to give you all the benefit of the doubt and accept that it was possibly a terrible accident and not deliberate. Nevertheless,' he went on, 'you were all disgustingly drunk and out of bounds in the kitchens.' He paused and whispered something to the adjutant alongside him before clearing his throat and adding, 'I don't know the identity of the perpetrator who killed the poor cat – only he himself knows that, and he will have to live with it. Unfortunately, I'm left with no alternative but to find you all guilty. I sentence all of you to twenty-eight days confined to barracks, with nightly guard duties. And,' he went on in an angry voice, 'you should all be thoroughly ashamed of yourselves for your disgusting behaviour.' Then we were quick-marched out to serve our sentences. With the benefit of hindsight, we got off quite lightly. If we had been pulled up in front of one of the old Uxbridge bullshitters, it would have been even money for a long spell in the glasshouse!

I didn't mind the nightly guard duties, but four weeks stuck in this dump would be hard to handle. But as time went by, so the funny incidents started to happen, especially at weekends when it seemed that we were the only people on the camp. During the week, the NAAFI was the place to have a laugh. All the guys used to gather there and have a few bevvies. And during the week, *all* the NAAFI girls seemed quite pretty and game for a giggle. Of course, the guys' testosterone was bubbling up and they were always on the lookout for a conquest, but the competition was fierce. But what a difference at weekends. It appeared that the pretty NAAFI girls all went back home to their husbands and boyfriends and we were lumbered with one really fat and ugly NAAFI girl called Florence. Naturally, being cruel and a bit boozy at the time, we shortened her name to match the safe anchorage used by the Imperial Fleet in the First World War – fat Florence became 'Scapa Flo'!

In maturity, I now sadly realise that Florence was someone's loving daughter and probably had a Mum and Dad who doted on her. But we were young, very flash and very shallow, and never even considered that she might have been a very nice girl. In our eyes, she was fat and ugly and we were very fond of saying, 'I wouldn't touch her with a bargepole, no matter how desperate I was.' But it's a funny old world, isn't it? Come the second weekend of loneliness and no conquests, and after downing a few pints and maybe a short or two, Scapa Flo was not looking so fat any more. That once ugly girl had, with the able assistance of a massive intake of alcohol, magically transformed into a big, buxom, sexy lady, and suddenly there were half a dozen of us sniffing around and trying to 'get on the firm'. I often have a chuckle to myself when I think about the antics

Buzzing the control tower – a scene oft repeated at airfields across England during the war. This is an American Fortress with 'nothing on the clock but the maker's name', as the line shoot went. *(RAF Museum, Hendon)*

we got up to with Scapa Flo. She was loving every minute of it, and why not – she had the pick of the bunch, with no competition in sight! Scout's honour, it definitely wasn't me who scored with Scapa Flo at the death! Mind you, it was a close cockney mate of mine who made it and he never lived it down after re-entering the world from his drunken stupor! From that fateful day to the end of his service, he was always known as the man who had bravely 'torpedoed' the pride of RAF Bassingbourn, Scapa Flo. I think the relevant citation hanging proudly in our hut read thus: 'Bravery above and beyond the call of duty'!

My mate who had had his wicked way with Scapa Flo was a bit of a DJ and did some evening sessions on Radio Bassingbourn. We were forever persuading him to play the popular Eartha Kitt number 'Santa Baby', especially after the BBC had banned it for its sexual undertones and the inference that this young girl was singing about her lecherous old sugar daddy as Santa Claus. We would all lie on our bunks when the record came on, swigging away on our many beers and shouting out the words.

The words definitely had double meanings, and with Eartha Kitt putting the sexual emphasis into it, it was a right giggle. But once again one of the Holy Joes complained to the CO and the song was taken off our hit list, much to our disgust and annoyance! The words went something like this . . .

Santa baby, just slip a sable under the tree for me;
Been an awful good girl, Santa baby,
So hurry down the chimney tonight. . . .

Think of all the fun I've missed,
Think of all the fellas that I haven't kissed;
Next year I could be just as good
If you'll check off my Christmas list. . . .

Hurry down the chimney tonight,
Hurry . . . tonight.

So, finally, I had done my 'jankers' and I was now allowed to go home again at weekends. By this time I had managed to research the practice of getting to London at a cheap rate, and I had got it down to a fine art. Key to my success were the fruit and veg lorries, loaded with fine East Anglian produce, that headed for Covent Garden every Friday evening. The trouble was that I had an early chit for Saturday mornings, but I solved that problem with ease by bribing the guys who I knew were on Friday night guard duties. It only took a pack of American snout and they were quite happy to turn their backs while I went over the wire. As for all the lorry drivers who stopped to give me a lift, well, another two packs of American snout did the trick – it was like manna from heaven for them. In fact, I became so well known among the drivers on that particular route, that one of my regulars used to stop by the wire and wait for me to emerge at a given time! They took me all the way to King's Cross, which was just a short walk from my home.

So I'd get the train from Waterloo every Saturday and play my part-time pro soccer in the old Southern League. We'd attract a crowd of three or four hundred and I would have the shit kicked out of me by the old pros who hated us youngsters. But I'd pick up three quid after the match for my bruises, an extra pound if we won and half a quid if we drew. I know it sounds a pittance by today's standards, but that three quid was exactly twice as much as my whole week's wages in the RAF! And that three quid on top of my wages enabled me to live the life of Riley at Bassingbourn. I paid one of the guys to make my bed, another to iron my uniform and yet another to clean my kit on the very rare occasions when a bullshit-minded warrant officer passed through the camp in transit. But these old bull-shitters didn't last too long with our keen groupie. They interfered with his schedule of day and night flying, and he soon had them shipped out.

The major part of my dough went on Saturday night boozing at the Tottenham Royal, the Hornsey Town Hall or the Lyceum in the Strand. I must tell you this great story about one of our mates we used to drink with at the old Hornsey Town Hall. His name was Terry Parsons and he was 'on the buses' as a driver at the Archway depot. Now, Terry had a great voice and had a regular spot singing at the Favourite Pub in Hornsey Rise. As luck would have it, one Saturday night we were all up the Hornsey Town Hall having a good booze-up. The resident bandleader – if my memory serves me right, I think his name was Fred Davies – gave an announcement from the stage. It appeared that his singer had gone on the booze and was legless, and was there anyone in the audience who could give a decent song? So without any prompting, we pushed Terry up onto the stage. The rest is just magic history. Terry went down a treat with his wonderful voice and was promptly signed up as a regular at the town hall.

And it didn't end there. One of the most famous and influential bandleaders of that era, Joe Loss, came sniffing around because he could spot talent. He signed Terry up, and changed his name to Matt Monro, Matt after one of the studio musicians and Monro after the great Winifred

Atwell's dad. So our old mate had become a world-famous singing sensation almost overnight! Even the late great Frank Sinatra reckoned Matt Monro was probably the very best male vocalist that Britain had ever produced. But Terry was never happy with the British public as he believed that he didn't get the plaudits he deserved. I recall a time when I was dropping off a fare at Heathrow Airport and I noticed Terry unloading his big flash American car. I shouted out to him, 'Alright, Tel?' He looked up as I sped past and shouted back, 'I ain't been called that name for years, Alf.' Sadly, Terry died far too young after picking up a terrible virus on one of his African tours. What an awful waste of such God-given talent. It's strange what fate gives out, isn't it? Fame and fortune on the one hand and a kick up the whatsits on the other!

Anyway, the remainder of my dosh went on taking out the 'Richards' (Richard the Third, bird – get it?). Sadly, my recent experiences of being banged-up at Bassingbourn for a whole month on jankers obviously hadn't taught me a lesson. Any other sensible person in my situation would have kept their head down and played it cool for a while. But no, not me. I was home again for the weekend, and after playing for my Southern League soccer team in the afternoon and earning a 'massive' four pounds, including an extra pound for a win bonus, I had money to burn! The youngsters of today may well snigger at my calling four quid a massive amount of money. But I'm talking half a century ago and my RAF weekly pay was only a measly thirty bob a week. So I had earned more than double that amount on a Saturday afternoon just for having the shit kicked out of me by the old pros, much to the delight of a smattering of masochistic home supporters! Let's be fair, you'd have to be a masochist to stand out in the cold, freezing your cods off watching a bunch of young kids like me and a gaggle of has-beens chasing a football over a surface of cloying, clinging mud. By the time any player had even managed to reach the penalty area, they were too knackered by the mud to attempt a shot. It was all they could do to stand up!

That four quid went a long way in the early 1950s, believe me. The best seats in the back of the pics, where the lads went for a grope with their girlfriends, only cost one and nine pence. It didn't cost much more than that to get into a dance hall – about half a crown. If you reckon on a pint of beer at about five pence, a packet of ciggies costing the same and a massive bag of fish and chips at about ten pence, only then can today's youngsters begin to comprehend the spending value of the dough in my pocket.

So, it was Saturday evening, my juices were rising and I was feeling every inch a stallion and raring to go! That meant putting on my best 'whistle' (whistle and flute, suit), then meeting my mates at the bus stop by the Cally Baths on Caledonian Road and hopping on to a trolley bus up to the Tottenham Royal Dance Hall. For those too young to know what a trolley bus is, or was, they were all electric and got their power from the two huge conductor poles that clamped onto overhead wires. Everything ran nice and quiet on the 'trolleys', and they were very effective as buses until such times as they reached a major overhead junction like the Nag's Head, with wires criss-crossing every which way.

If the driver was going just a fraction too fast at this junction, there would suddenly be an almighty crash and the two huge poles would come off and start flapping down the side of the bus. They looked like the two legs of some giant bird that had just been shot! Out would get the driver and the conductor and, going to the rear of the vehicle, they would proceed to pull out this huge long pole from under the body of the bus. At the end of this huge long pole was a huge hook, and the object of the exercise was to hook the two huge poles one at a time and attempt to replace them on the overhead electric wires. That's when the fun started – especially if it was pouring with rain and blowing a gale, as it was on this particular evening. All of us lads would lower the windows for a giggle and shout out false directions to the bloke wobbling about like a demented pole-vaulter who couldn't find his bar! 'A little to the right, John', we'd yell, or, 'Up a bit mate, no, no, down a bit, you've missed it again, you plonker.' Then we'd all fall back on our seats curled up with laughter, while the poor old conductor was getting drenched to the skin. This was the Achilles' heel of the trolley buses and possibly the main cause of their being condemned to the scrap heap after a relatively short working life.

Finally, and after much cheering, the poles found their power again and off we 'hummed'. A few minutes later, we heard some sounds of squelching shoes coming up the stairs and the rain-sodden conductor approached us for our fares. He was a little old boy sporting a rather wet, drooping grey moustache and he looked positively pissed off, but still we gave him some stick. One of the lads piped up with a big grin on his face,

'I didn't fink it was raining out there Alfie, did you?' We all giggled like a bunch of kids and I replied, 'I would have thought if you got a job as a bus conductor, you'd never expect to get wet, would you?' The old boy didn't say a word while we all curled up again with laughter. He just sniffed, pulled on his damp moustache in an everyday mannerism and rang the bell three times. 'Okay, clever-arses,' he shouted out as he disappeared down the stairs, 'this bus ain't moving until you mob get off, or I'll call the police to have you thrown off.' And that, as they say in the movies, was checkmate. The other passengers were glaring at us in the irritation of being delayed and we had no alternative. So four flash yobbos were forced to eat humble pie, run the gauntlet of a bus full of irate passengers and beat a hasty retreat. As we clattered down the stairs in acute embarrassment, we had to pass the old conductor on the platform and, quite naturally, he gave us back some stick. 'I think you'll find it's still pissing down out there, lads. But not to worry, with your big 'eads the rain won't reach your whistles!' He chuckled at his own humour and shouted out after us, 'With a fair bit of luck, there might be annuvver bus come along tonight!' Be fair, we deserved everything we got!

Some time later and rather damp, we arrived at the Tottenham Royal. It was straight down to the bar for something to keep out the cold and some time to relax. And before long the alcohol had started to kick in and we were actually laughing about the incident on the bus. But have you ever experienced that certain feeling some days that fate is going to deal you a dodgy sort of hand? That's exactly how I felt. I couldn't put my finger on it, but I just felt that our night out had started a bit iffy and I had this feeling that it might well get 'iffier'. And how right I was. By this time we were pleasantly sozzled, so we decided to try our luck in the dance hall. I recall that in those far-off days at the edge of the dance floor were these rather large, imitation stone pedestals, about 4ft in height and used as very large ashtrays. The other three blokes were off 'hunting' and I was leaning casually against one of these pedestals trying to chat up this pretty young girl. To this very day I'm still not too sure what really happened next. This man-mountain of a guy, built, as they say in the forces, like a brick shit-house, suddenly emerged from nowhere, grabbed me by the scruff of the neck, and snarled, 'Wot's your effing game chatting up my bird?' Thankfully the 'cavalry' arrived in the shape of my mate Del Boy, who was totally fearless and promptly whacked this man-mountain on the hooter with a vicious right-hander. Then all hell broke loose, and the whole of the dance floor seemed to join in the fracas. The girls started screaming, people were running in all directions, and others came to join in the punch-up. I copped a couple of nasty right-handers from a bloke who must have been a friend of the big fella, and Del Boy was floored by another geezer. The last thing I remember was feeling as though a horse had kicked me on the back of the head, and I went spark out!

I had these blurry visions of a copper talking to me, then it was a bloke in a white coat feeling my head and a nurse washing my face. But it was all dream-like and unreal. When I finally returned to this planet I found myself banged-up in a police cell – not for the first time! My head was thumping like mad, there was claret all over my new shirt, and my expensive whistle looked like it had come off a rag-and-bone cart! Mind you, my mate Del Boy didn't look too clever either. His boat race looked as though a demented Spanish dancer had used it to stamp out a fiendish flamenco! I suppose one could describe it very loosely as a 'Union-Jack Face' – all red, white and blue. Even in adversity I liked a good laugh. I called across to Del Boy and said, 'Did you have a good night, mate?' He grinned and mumbled through his swollen lips, 'Yeah, Alf, I've 'ad a blinding time.' But behind the shallow humour, I knew I was in deep shit. I needed to get back to Bassingbourn by early Monday morning, otherwise I'd be listed as AWOL, and that meant being put on yet another charge.

There was the sound of keys grating in the lock, the cell door opened, and in came a friendly looking old custody sergeant. 'This is the latest news,' he said with a broad grin on his face. 'It's Sunday lunchtime and you two flash gits have been spark out for nearly twelve hours in my cells. Tomorrow you will both appear at Tottenham Magistrates Court charged with being drunk and disorderly and causing an affray. The other guy concerned – apparently he's a well-known local professional wrestler – is pressing charges for assault and battery against both of you.' Would you Adam-and-Eve it, I thought. Out of all the pretty girls in the Tottenham Royal, I had to try and chat up the girlfriend of a bloody professional wrestler built like a brick shit-house; what a wally! Mind you, I could try my luck as a fortune-teller in the future. I'd known something was afoot at the start of our night out.

So that was that. We were due up in front of the 'beak' the next day and there was absolutely nothing I could do about it. Maybe not – but perhaps

I could chat up the old custody sergeant, give him the sob-story and perhaps cross his palm. It was worth a try. 'Can I have a word with you, Sarge?' I asked. He nodded, and I proceeded to tell him my problem of desperately needing to get back to my camp by the next morning. 'I'm sorry, lad,' he replied, 'but you should have thought of that before you started punching like Joe Louis.' He went towards the cell door, and turning around, said, 'I'd like to help, lad, but it's out of my hands because you've already been charged.' With that he left the cell, and me and my mate crashed out on our bunks right through to the next day.

After a wash and brush-up and a bit of breakfast, we were led to the Black Maria and transported to the court. We were the first case up and we all had to stand up when the lady magistrate appeared. She was a really big lady, and I reckoned that her bosom was quite capable of smothering a parliament of owls! The magistrate must have been up bright and early for her visit to the hairdressers. Her Marcel waving, all the rage with mature ladies of the day, was so severe and pronounced, it made me feel a little sea-sick. She peered at us through her pince-nez specs as though we were something nasty stuck to the bottom of her shoes. Luckily for us, the man-mountain hadn't appeared to press charges. My mate reckoned we had frightened him off, so that was one charge of A&B dropped from the file. The lady with the big boobs spoke after looking down at the charges. 'I've got to fine you two people,' she said in a rather masculine voice, 'but your awful appearance looks as though you were the victims and not the aggressors.' I think we got off quite lightly with a few quid in fines and bound over to keep the peace.

That wasn't a problem. My problem was attempting to sneak back into camp on Monday afternoon without being spotted. I hoped and prayed that my mates had managed to cover for me, but I was bang out of luck. That Monday, out of all the Mondays in the year, some old bullshit-conscious flight sergeant, who was only in transit anyway, had pulled in a couple of my mates after breakfast for looking 'scruffy'. That's a joke in itself – everyone stationed at Bassingbourn was scruffy! Anyway, this old 'Flight' took it upon himself to visit our quarters, check our tidiness – which was abysmal – and have a head-count. I heard later that the head-count had taken him nearly an hour, because my mates deliberately added one to his count every time they returned from the loo. If only we had thought of making up a big lifelike dummy, just like in the war film

Albert RN, then we might have got away with the deception! Finally he got it right and discovered he was one short in the billet. 'So who's missing?' the chaps told me he had asked suspiciously. 'Bootsie' took it upon himself to try and confuse the old bullshitter. 'Well, sir,' said Bootsie, 'I believe AC2 Townsend has been posted to another station nearer his home on compassionate grounds, but it's all happened so quickly, sir, nobody's quite sure of where he's gone.'

But the game was up. The flight sergeant, with all his vast experience, knew that there was something fishy going on and he only needed to check the postings in the adjutant's office to confirm his suspicions. When I eventually arrived at the main gate, he was lurking in the guardroom waiting for me. I knew the sentry on the gate, and any other time I could probably have sneaked in undetected. But I could tell from the nervous look in his eyes directed in the direction of the guardroom that the game was up. He checked my papers and, after whispering to me, 'Sorry, mate', he yelled out in a loud voice for the benefit of the lurking flight sergeant. 'You are twelve hours overdue, Airman, and it is my duty to inform you that you will be placed on a charge.' Then out came the old bullshitter with a big smile on his face. 'Take this airman to the guardroom cells,' he instructed the sentry. 'He will be charged with being AWOL in the morning.' So it was out of one nick and into another!

There was absolutely no point in making excuses when I was double-marched in front of the CO. The deep frown on his face and the look of annoyance told me from the off that he recognised me from my recent indiscretions. I hadn't thrown the old moggy into the scalding water, but I was still one of the gang who were involved. 'You simply can't treat this camp as a hotel of convenience or some sort of cheap bed and breakfast accommodation, laddie,' he said testily, while looking down at some papers on his desk. 'I would have thought you'd learned your lesson after that dreadful incident in the cookhouse, but apparently you seem to think that you can come and go whenever you please. It's just not on, laddie, and I won't stand for it.' He went into a deep huddle with the adjutant sitting beside him, and I remember thinking once more what a wonderful mop of grey hair he had. I always think silly things when I'm nervous! Finally, he looked up and said angrily, 'Your face looks in a terrible state and you're a damn disgrace to the RAF. Report to the MO and for God's sake get yourself cleaned up.' He paused, and continued wearily, 'I sentence you to twenty-eight days confined to camp, with nightly guard duties.' Then, wagging his finger at me in a threatening manner, he almost shouted, 'I'm giving you a final warning – and pass it on to all the other reprobates in your billet. The very next time you or one of your cronies appears in front of me, I'll throw the damn book at all of you.' Finally, waving his arms in irritation and with his eyes almost popping out in frustration, he yelled, 'Get this bloody airman out of my sight, Sergeant!' With that, it was a sloppy salute from me and I was quick-marched out to start another session of jankers. So, what's new?

The nightly guard duties weren't a problem for me. Once the guard commander had done his nightly rounds and gone back to bed, the rest of us crashed out in the guardroom! Again, it was the weekends that killed me, more so this time around because I didn't have my mates doing time with me. All of them were off on their weekend passes and the only people left on camp were the sad, lonely ones who didn't have any relatives or friends – or even a home. Tragically, their only home was the RAF and that's probably why they had signed on in the first place. For sure I had some sympathy with these guys, but some of them were really weird and I felt uncomfortable among them in the NAAFI. The word on the grapevine was that most of them were 'fairies', as gays were cruelly called in those days. Even some of the NAAFI girls wouldn't talk to me at the weekends because they thought I was one of them! It didn't end there, either. When all the lads returned on Monday, I got some stick from them as well. 'Alright, mate?' they would ask with a wicked laugh. 'Did you 'ave a good time with all those "iron-hoofs"?' which is rhyming slang for, you know who! I could take it from my mates, but only from my mates.

Then a couple of new faces arrived on the scene in our billet, which helped to alleviate my utter boredom. These were a couple of Jewish 'bad-lads', who allegedly had been involved in a scam at another station's stores. The word was that plenty of gear had gone 'astray', but because of all the different guys working in the stores on a temporary basis, the military police had had trouble nicking the culprit – or culprits. But Morris and Emmanuel had some 'form' and were posted on the premise that it was probably them; proving it was another matter. Having been dragged up among a closely knit cockney circle, I'd never had much experience of Jews and I wasn't really anti-Semitic, or anti anything. I can recall my mates chiding me many years ago for doing my old Mum's shopping in Levy's fruit and vegetable shop up the Caledonian Road. 'You don't wanna spend your money there, Alfie,' they'd say, ''cos he's a yid.' 'So what's a yid?' I would enquire innocently. Then they'd prattle on about guys who had big beards and who wore funny clothes in a synagogue when they prayed. 'I reckon our old vicar must be a bit funny as well,' I'd reply, ''cos he wears what looks like a woman's white frock in church!' I remember Mr Levy smiling at me after hearing the embarrassing conversation and saying, 'You'll make a fine father when you grow up, my boy.'

Morris and Emmanuel were both East End boys through and through. If ever you were looking for a couple of smart operators on your market stall in Petticoat Lane, or any other market, these two would fit the bill. Talk about plenty of chat and spiel – all the boys reckoned they could flog winter overcoats to people in the tropics! Morris was a big bloke with a rather prominent nose. He looked a dead ringer for the world-famous singer Tony Bennett. But he did like a gossip and you never told Morris any secrets. Because of this failing we shortened his name to 'Mo' and nicknamed him 'Mo the Grass'. That nickname still tickles me! As for Emmanuel, who liked to be called Manny, his surname was Mercer. So in honour of the great Joe Mercer, captain of Arsenal and England at that time, he was called 'Joe'. What I admired about these two guys was their great Jewish humour and their cunning and intricate ways of always trying to beat the system. Let me give you an example. One of my pet hates of a weekend – a pet hate of any bad lad – was church parades. We all had to line up on parade every week while a snotty nosed young corporal would give the order: 'Jews and other denominations, two paces forward and dismiss.' So Mo the Grass and Joe Mercer, with a big grin on their faces, would take two paces forward – and disappear! The rest of us, many – including myself – who didn't have a clue what our religion was about, had to suffer the incredibly boring sermons of this batty old padre who used to prattle on and on concerning 'Moses in the bullrushes who was hiding from some evil king called Herod'. The boys used to pour out of the church afterwards, light up a ciggie and say things like, 'I 'ope that King bleedin' 'Erod finds that bloke in the bull's whatsits by next week, or I'll go round the twist!'

The whole idea of dismissing 'Jews and other denominations' from the intolerable church parades was so that they could go and pray in their own holy places. But the RAF, in their infinite wisdom, never had any mosques or synagogues on the camp. So all the Jews and other denominations had beaten the system. That was until the batty old padre was pensioned off and we had a bright young padre come on board. Imagine the utter surprise on the faces of Mo and Joe when he called on them one day in our billet and asked them where they prayed! Their ensuing replies can only be described as absolute classics. Now we're talking here about two streetwise East Enders whose closest visit to any synagogue was the Blind Beggars pub in Whitechapel Road! And their complex tales of trying to get enough cash together so that they could satisfy a lifelong dream of visiting 'the Holy Land' had us nearly wetting ourselves. The farthest east these two scallywags had ever travelled was to the market in Clacton-on-Sea to flog some dodgy gear! And yet they succeeded in convincing the young padre that they always used the solitude of the empty billet to pray to their god. What a classic performance!

This business about church parades seemed to spark some bright ideas from a billet of scallywags. The thinking was, if Mo and Joe could beat the system, then why couldn't we? My twenty-eight days of jankers was nearly complete, but the threat of the dreaded church parades lingered on, especially with the arrival of a brand new corporal. The conniving brain of my mate Bootsie was onto it like a flash. 'This new geezer taking church parades ain't got a clue who's who, has he, Alf?' he said to me, knowingly. 'So,' he went on, 'what if a couple of us tried it on and pretended we were other denominations, do you think he'd tumble it?' I thought long and hard about it before replying, 'You don't look a bit like a Jew,' I said, 'and me with my broken nose could never pass as one.' He thought for a moment before saying, 'Yeah, but if it came a tumble we could say we've been converted to something like Buddhism, or born-again Christians.' But I really didn't want to get involved, because if I got tumbled I'd be a three-time loser and maybe get sent to a bad-boys' glasshouse. That would add time on to my national service and was a definite no-no.

Suddenly, and not too soon, I'd done my time and I had a week's leave due to me. On my return I discovered that Bootsie and the twins from West Ham, Tom and Tim, aptly named 'Sex' and 'Violence' as Tom was sex-mad, while Tim wanted to whack everybody, had been nicked for pulling the scam on the church parades. The brand new corporal had been duped for a while, but when the bright, young padre had happened to turn up one day to check out the progress of his 'flock', just after my three mates had taken 'two paces forward', they were very quickly taken to the CO and dealt with accordingly because he didn't believe one little word of their conversion to any of those other religions!

Meanwhile, I was finding it harder and harder to motivate myself to get back on that train every Sunday evening, especially if I was 'in love' again, which was quite often! Then, suddenly, I heard on the grapevine of a little scam that might just help me solve my problem.

The 'Bent' Doctor

Every single guy in our hut was crooked, slippery and always on the look-out for 'clues'. But by far the top man and the guy who guided us with our misdemeanours was little, inoffensive Bootsie with his choirboy looks, who appeared for all the world as though butter wouldn't melt in his mouth. From the off we had nicknamed him 'Bootsie', because he had convinced the MO that his feet were so bad he should be 'excused boots'. He would wander around the camp in white plimsolls, and when he got a 'pull' from one of the senior NCOs he'd pull out his 'excused-boots chit' and stick it under their noses defiantly! Incidentally, this nickname was conceived long before the BBC scriptwriters had used it in their successful comedy series about life in the army. In fact, the cunning and clever Bootsie had a chit for just about every ailment including, would you believe, Sunday church parades. His excuse? Standing still for too long made him feel nauseous! He had this almost cherubic face and wouldn't say boo to a goose, yet he was the best licker of arses it's ever been my privilege to see. I saw him suck up to young officers and newly made-up NCOs and convince them utterly that he wasn't fit enough to do this job or that job.

He got very pissed off one day about having to carry this big vacuum cleaner around. So in front of all the guys and the young corporal in charge, he suddenly screamed out in pain and collapsed dramatically on the floor complaining of his 'old problem', a hernia. We rushed across to help him, trying hard not to laugh, while the young corporal tried to get him to his feet, asking anxiously, 'You alright, mate, better go over to the NAAFI, get yourself a cuppa, then go and have a lie-down.' We were all staring down at the floor in fits of giggles, while Bootsie started to ham it up something rotten in front of a captive audience. He limped slowly 'in agony' towards the door, then turned round, saying, 'I've suffered with this for years but I never complain, because I try and pull my weight with the rest of the lads.' He continued his 'agonised' shuffle towards the door and then, with a final thespian flourish with one hand, he said to the young and now very worried-looking corporal, 'It's a real pleasure to meet a real gentleman and I'm positive they won't be your last stripes during your service. Thank you kindly for being a real human being.' Then Bootsie made his exit 'stage left' to rapturous applause from his appreciative audience! By the time we had finished our duties and got back to our hut, Bootsie was spark out on the bed. What a performer!

Suddenly, though, Bootsie was on the missing list. He hadn't returned from a weekend pass and the guys were concerned that maybe he'd gone on the run. A full week went by and still there was no sign of that cherubic face. Midway through the second week, in he strolled while we were having a pint in the NAAFI. 'You 'ad a problem, mate?' I enquired. He looked at me with his innocent and almost angelic face and smiled the smile he always used when conning people. 'Yeah mate,' he replied, 'I've 'ad this terrible viral flu and I've been flat on my back for nearly two weeks.' Now, Bootsie lived near me up the Angel, Islington, and I'd heard a whisper that he'd been seen more than once with a bird in the Spanish Patriots pub in Chapel Market. All us locals called it by its nickname of 'The Pats'. So, ever so casually, I said to him, 'So you weren't even well enough to go out for a drink then, mate?' 'Christ no, Alf,' he spluttered. 'I could hardly lift myself up in bed, mate, I really fought I was a gonner I'll tell you.' Now I was certain he was conning me, as I had seen that performance many times before. So I suddenly grabbed him by the scruff of his collar and whispered in his ear with feeling, 'You're a lying little bastard, Bootsie, 'cos you've been seen with a bird in The Pats, what d'ya say to that?' He took a quick gulp of his pint and grinned at me with a twinkle in those big blue eyes, knowing full well that he had been rumbled. He cast a twitchy, anxious glance behind him and whispered back, 'For Gawd's sake, Alf, keep this under your hat or we'll finish up in the nick.' He took another nervous glance behind him before saying, 'Here's the full story. One of the local villains told me he's got this old doctor straightened up 'cos the doc's partial to a little bit of bent gear.

So,' he continued to whisper, 'the villain puts the squeeze on the doc and asks for a moody sick certificate for his bruvver who's in the forces.' 'Okay, you cunning little bastard, so where do you come in?' I enquired. 'Use your noddle, Alf,' he said. 'I'm the bleedin' bruvver ain't I, and I copped the moody sick certificate.'

I leaned back in my chair with a large grin on my face. This could well be my answer to the weekly boredom of national service. Let's look at it as extended paid leave, I thought. 'That's a cracking scam, Bootsie,' I said. 'Now, are you going to put your old mates on the firm?' 'I can put *you* on the firm, Alf,' he said, 'because you're from the same manor as me. But,' he explained quietly, 'if I include the other guys from all over the place, we'll finish up getting nicked.' I sat back and considered what he said. He talked a lot of sense, did Bootsie. If I remember rightly, when you were doing your national service you never had a regular GP. So the North London lads could go to this bent doctor up the Angel if they were feeling a bit iffy. But if we put the South London boys on the firm, it might well come a tumble and we'd all fall! This needed some planning.

So, before my next weekend pass I bashed Bootsie's ear for the name and address of the bent doctor. After another boozy weekend I turned up at this scruffy little surgery in Essex Road first thing on Monday morning, and when it was my turn I went into the surgery coughing – with feeling! The doctor was an old Asian guy and probably near retirement age, and his breath definitely smelled as though he'd been taking some of his 'special medicine' in his private room! He shuffled across to me, took my pulse, and said, 'So, you are a friend of Big Mick?' 'Yeah, that's right, doc,' I replied. 'And,' he went on, 'I believe you are serving in the RAF, is that correct?' 'Yeah that's right, doc,' I replied for the second time. 'And you have got a terrible cough and you are feeling feverish?' he enquired. 'And you are not fit to return to your camp, is that correct?' Again, I said, 'Yeah, that's right, doc' because he was putting the answers into my mouth. He went back to his desk and started writing out a prescription. 'Take this medicine three times a day,' he said, 'then come back to see me in a week's time.' Then, without even batting an eyelid, he said, 'That will be ten shillings.' I had half a mind to call him a cheating old git. But what the hell, it had cost me half a quid and I was still a pound in front on my wages – and I now had an extra week at home! In fact, I stretched it to nearly two weeks! During that time, being a bit short of readies, I got myself a little job down Porters the Brewers, who used to have a factory in Crinan Street near King's Cross. No cards, no tax and paid up front in readies. I went back to the bent doctor some ten days later and he had the audacity to enquire about my bad cough! 'Well, Doc,' I said, coughing lightly, 'I fink I'm getting better, but maybe I might need an excused-duties chit to help me back on my feet.' He peered at me balefully from behind his big horn-rimmed specs and went back to his desk to write something. 'Take this chit back to your CO,' he said, 'and tell him you're to be on light duties until your chest gets a bit stronger. And,' he went on, 'I would suggest that your cough shouldn't deteriorate for at least one month. Do you understand what I am saying?' I nodded in reply. This was one cunning old dog who knew his way around the block. What a diabolical liberty, I thought – even my chit cost me another ten bob!

I was in for another shock when I returned to camp, because our hut was half a dozen short in personnel. My mucker, Half-Pint from Bermondsey, was off 'sick', as were the twins from West Ham, 'Sex' and 'Violence'. Also missing again was our mentor Bootsie, plus Nobby Clark and Chalky White. We would all be in deep shit if the CO compared the signatures on the sick notes! Luckily for us, a major flu epidemic was striking down much of the population at this juncture. So for the moment we were safe, but unless we thought about our scam in more detail we'd all finish up in the glasshouse. As per usual, the cunning and resourceful Bootsie came up with a workable solution. We'd go sick in strict rotation and not all at the same time.

This system worked pretty well for a time, then unfortunately one of our firm cocked it up. The diminutive Half-Pint, of all people, had got the hots for a bird and he was feeling too randy to wait. So he went 'sick' out of turn and completely cocked-up the scam. At long last, the CO tumbled the same doctor's signature on all of the sick notes. He knew full well that a fiddle was going on, but trying to prove it was another matter. So he did the next best thing by issuing this order on the notice board in an effort to curb the abuse. The wording went something like this:

IT HAS COME TO MY NOTICE THAT A CERTAIN
DOCTOR IN NORTH LONDON HAS BEEN ISSUING
SICK NOTES TO MY AIRMEN. IN FUTURE, ANY
SUCH SICK NOTES FROM THIS PARTICULAR DOCTOR

WILL BE CHECKED OUT BY THE STATION MO
WITH A THOROUGH MEDICAL EXAMINATION.
ANY AIRMAN FOUND TO BE PERFECTLY HEALTHY
WILL BE CHARGED ACCORDINGLY.

The message was loud and clear from the CO: he had tumbled our scam, and if we ignored his warning we'd all get nicked. The trouble with doing time in the glasshouse was that time spent in the nick was added on to your service time. Some of the real hard nuts finished up going twice my time in national service! Suffice to say, we all took the hint. It had been a good scam while it lasted. But all good things come to an end, and the successful villains are those who can predict the possible end of a good thing. As for the old bent doctor, I heard on the grapevine that he had also been tumbled a couple of years later and struck off by the BMA.

I often sit and chuckle at some of the diabolical scams we pulled just to skive from our RAF duties. It was always Bootsie who was our mentor. I often wonder whatever happened to him – God only knows! He's either finished up doing time in the nick, or made a million with some shady deals. He was a very shrewd, lovely bloke, and I've got this sneaky feeling that he's made bundles!

HALFWAY TO CIVVY STREET

Over a period of time, I had adjusted to life in the RAF. To be perfectly honest, if you didn't learn to adapt it could drive you round the bend. We all loved watching the gangster movies and we all used the expression 'stir-crazy', which actually related to long-term prisoners. But actually *being* stir-crazy, which in effect meant going mad because you wanted to get out, was a serious problem with some of the young airmen, especially the 'Mummy's Boys', who often cried themselves to sleep at night.

As I said earlier, our little firm was at the very bottom of the RAF ladder in terms of ambition and promotion. We were literally marking time until we'd finished our stint. Consequently, we got all the crappy jobs that nobody else in their right mind would think of doing. For example, we were called out late one evening because a depressed and homesick young airman had somehow got himself a gun, put the barrel into his mouth, pulled the trigger, and blown his effing brains all over the toilet wall! The ever-resourceful Bootsie started the ball rolling by saying to the corporal in charge of the clean-up operation, 'I'm sorry, mate, but I wouldn't clean up this crap for a score a week. So I ain't gonna to do it for effing thirty bob a week.' 'Watch your mouth, airman,' said the young corporal, who was looking a bit green around the gills. Now Bootsie was a past master at spotting the slightest chink in anyone's armour, and he had seen that the young corporal was feeling a little 'Tom and Dick' at the sight of all the blood and brains spattered over the wall. 'I'll tell you what, Corp,' he said, with a big grin on his face, 'how d'ya fancy a nice greasy bacon sarnie after we've cleared up?' That did it. The young corporal pulled out his hanky, held it to his mouth, and rushed out of the toilet post-haste! So instead of wiping everything off by hand, as instructed, we carted in a large hosepipe and flooded the place out in five minutes flat!

Another evening, we were all sitting in the mess having our grub when the duty officer came in, stood on a table, and informed us that one of the young pilots had crashed a Canberra jet in the vicinity. He continued, 'I'm asking for volunteers to search for the bodies.' I had never volunteered for anything in the RAF, but this was something different. Somewhere out there in the pitch blackness of the night were three human beings – the young pilot, the navigator and the instructor – maybe still alive and seriously injured. So we all piled into some trucks and went bumping down dirt tracks to where the plane had crashed. Now it was my turn to feel Tom and Dick when I saw the massive crater caused by the Canberra jet. The whole dreadful scene came alive again many decades later when I saw the Lockerbie crater on television. Nobody, but nobody, could survive that crash, I thought to myself.

Tragically, I was proven correct and the officers in charge of the crash site instructed us to look out for pieces of bodies. They brought out three coffins in the glare of the spotlights and filled these up with any bits and pieces found on the site. All the guys were a bit squeamish, but I was worse than most. No way could I pick up pieces of human beings, even though I didn't find any. The futile search was called off after a couple of hours. I noticed the officers putting some rocks into the three coffins, presumably to make them weigh as much as bodies. Full military funerals were held a week or so later, but tragically that wasn't the end of the sad affair. The following month it was rumoured in the camp that the torso of one of the crew had been found behind a hedge by a local farmer. This had

Some Canberras are still flying with the RAF at the beginning of the twenty-first century – not bad for a plane that first entered service in the early 1950s. *(RAF Museum, Hendon)*

to be hushed up for obvious reasons, and whether it was fact or fiction I never did find out.

However, there was one particular duty that I didn't mind, and it was allocated on a rota system. About once a fortnight our hut had to collect red and green flags from the stores. Then, in shifts of two, we would take it in turns to head out to the little sentry boxes that were positioned either side of the flightpath on the once pretty, country lane. And, believe it or not, we used to lie down in the occasionally warm sun and wait for the phones to buzz. In this modern, high-tech age it's almost unbelievable that a crowd of layabouts like us could have held the destiny of a million-pound aircraft and, more importantly, the lives of three human beings in our hands! The system was very simple – in fact, it was positively primitive! When the phone did eventually buzz, we would grab our red and green flags and, provided that we weren't spark out, we'd rush out onto the road and stop the traffic. A few minutes later the Canberra jet bomber would come roaring in to land.

That was the theory anyway, but in practice it was totally different. You need to remember that all these pilots were young, nervous, inexperienced and often not very competent. They would often overshoot, and then we'd have to hold up all the traffic until the young pilots did another circuit and attempted another approach. I remember one fine summer's day when I was on road duty and the young pilot had overshot God knows how many times. Naturally, the lorry drivers were getting somewhat miffed at the delay. One of them who had a refrigerated vehicle shouted out mockingly in a very strong East Anglian accent to me and my mate, 'If the bugger doesn't get that plane down very soon, my full load of butter will be turning into bloody cheese!' We all had a laugh and enjoyed the joke because the young pilot was making a bit of a 'cow's arse' with his unsuccessful attempts at landing. But the boot was on the other foot a couple of minutes later, as it looked for all the world as though the plane's final approach was too low and it was going to plough into the lorries lined up below. So, working on the theory that discretion is the better part of valour, the lorry driver with all the 'rabbit' and his mates all opened their doors in absolute terror and dived headlong into the roadside ditch. They weren't alone in the soggy ditch, I might add, because me and my mucker had already dived in! The high-pitched, screaming roar from the powerful jet engines threatened to burst my eardrums, and holding a finger in either ear I sneaked a look up as the huge Canberra roared overhead. I swear to God that the plane missed the top of the lorries by just a matter of feet. I heard after the scare that the instructor had snatched the controls at the very last minute – what a way to earn a bloody living!

But apart from that incident, and a few more caused by the young airmen dropping off to sleep and not hearing the buzzer, it was a bit of a giggle out on the road with our red and green flags. It was also a great opportunity to cadge some beers from the brewery vans and some bread and cakes from the baker. But, best of all, it gave us the perfect chance to chat up some of the buxom country wenches as they sat waiting patiently

Oops! A collapsed undercarriage leg has made a mess of this Canberra . . .
(RAF Museum, Hendon)

on their bikes or in their cars. Can't you just picture the scenario? We were in total and absolute charge of the traffic and nobody, but nobody, moved until we said so – not even the bikes. I don't think any one of us has felt so important since! We'd strut along the line of traffic with our hands behind our backs, only stopping when we came across a pretty lady. My regular chat line was, 'I hope I'm not delaying you too long, my dear', while making sure I took in the fullness of her ample breasts. 'But,' I'd say, with a leer on my face, 'this is a very important job we're doing, and anything I do, I like to do properly!' If I got half a smile after that lecherous remark, I knew I could move on to asking her if she was married or courting and, most important, whether she lived locally. Finally, as a big favour, I could send her on her way before all the other traffic, but only if she had happened to succumb to my smooth chat-up line and agreed to meet me that evening in the local pub! The first couple of times, I have to admit I spent most of the evening by myself at the bar. But after much polishing-up of my approach, by including how 'famous' I was in the world of professional football, the nubile young ladies started to show.

I have a confession, though. Every single one of them turned up with their dads, who were mad-keen football supporters and only looking for the possibility of cup final tickets! As for me, the drinks cost me plenty of dough and the dads didn't offer to buy a round 'cos they considered themselves invited guests! To compound my frustrations, the pretty girls went home with their dads at closing time after a very cheap night out. What was that famous quote from the poet Robbie Burns about, 'The best-laid plans of mice and men'? Huh!

. . . after it swung off the runway. I hope the pilot had a good explanation for the wingco flying! *(RAF Museum, Hendon)*

The Final Countdown

After what seemed like a boring eternity, the time started to rush by and my service was due to be completed in a couple of months. I was still getting my regular early chits and sneaking under the wire every Friday evening. My football wages helped me to pay the guys who did my washing and ironing and cleaned my kit. But at this late stage, I didn't want to get involved in any scams or fiddles. In fact, I wanted to keep my nose squeaky clean and be the perfect airman. If I 'fell' and finished up doing time in the glasshouse with only a couple of months to go, that would be catastrophic and idiotic. So I became 'Mr Nice Guy' almost overnight, especially since many of my old mates in our hut had finished their time and had left with tearful farewells. Chalky White had gone, as had Sex and Violence. In fact, most of my old mates would be out before me, and there were already a lot of bright new faces in our hut being shown the ropes by the ever-resourceful Bootsie. As per usual, he had a scam going with the new recruits, who, like us many moons ago, were very gullible. He charged each and every one of them a small fee for his undoubted expertise in the art of skiving. It was money well spent to learn from such a 'master'!

Then, out of the blue, bloody disaster and a happening that would send our cosy little world into meltdown. The old CO had retired and the new CO, so we were informed, was heavy into bullshit and had brought along his own warrant officer to enforce it. We were all ordered to assemble on the parade ground to await nervously the opening speech from our new CO. As soon as he had mounted the rostrum, I whispered to Bootsie, 'This geezer's an arse-hole, he's gonna give us plenty of aggro.' Bootsie nodded wisely as the groupie, resplendent in his smart uniform, with a row of shiny medals on his chest and the 'scrambled egg' on his cap denoting his rank, started to speak. 'I've called you all here today to give you the opportunity to meet me,' he said, sounding for all the world like the old Prime Minister Sir Anthony Eden. 'As you may have heard,' he went on, 'in the very near future this station will no longer continue to be an OCU; in fact, it may well lose all of its aircraft and eventually be closed as an RAF establishment. So,' he continued, 'it will be my job and the job of warrant officer "Bloggs" over there to bring the place up to scratch because at the present time it's an absolute shambles.' I looked nervously across to where WO Bloggs was standing, and I didn't like the look of what I saw one little bit. It seemed as though my RAF experience could take on the dark and dismal shades of Uxbridge all over again. The clues all lay in the new WO's smartly pressed uniform, his glittering boots, and the peak of the hat flat against a nose that appeared to have absorbed plenty of left jabs in the past. He was a big man, maybe 6ft 3in, with a red, beefy face. This guy is trouble, I thought, and I need to stay well clear of him.

Suddenly, the new CO had gone and WO Bloggs made the rostrum shudder by clattering up the steps and saying in a thunderous voice, 'I've proudly served King and Queen and Country in the RAF for over twenty years and I've been posted to dozens of stations all over the world. But,' he went on in a menacing voice, 'I have never seen such a filthy dump as this and such a bloody shower as you lot out there.' He paused to take in some breath and, peering down on the parade trying desperately to make eye contact with some unfortunate erk trembling below him, he screamed out, 'Make no mistake about it, I intend making major changes just as soon as the flying is discontinued, and God help anyone who stands in my way.' Then he stomped down from the rostrum and marched smartly off the parade ground, leaving the rabble shuffling nervously at what might lie ahead for them in the uncertain future. Let's be honest, RAF Bassingbourn *was* a filthy dump and we *were* a bloody shower. But what with day and night flying, the old CO hadn't bothered with anything else. Now a new broom sweeping clean, with the assistance of an arse-hole WO, had put us deep in Shit Street.

I was now only weeks away from Civvy Street, and I certainly did not relish the thought of recruit-training bullshit all over again. I'd had it nice and cushy for almost two years, and that's the way I wanted it to stay for the remainder of my time. When we returned in stunned silence to our hut, Bootsie called me to one side and said, 'We're in deep trouble mate, 'ave you got any bright ideas to get us out of this shit?' Now luckily for me it was summertime, so I wasn't too bothered about losing the early chits 'cos I wasn't playing footie. 'Think about it, mate,' I said, 'the old CO's done a runner, so we can revert back to Plan A and go back to the bent doctor, without the new faces knowing what's going on.' Bootsie stared at the ground for what seemed like an eternity. Then he looked up and smiled his angelic smile, saying excitedly, 'That's brilliant, mate –

there's only a few of us old timers left and we can do that scam again without fear of being tumbled.' Bootsie had two weeks on the sick while flying was still in progress. Then another couple of the old timers in the hut had their turn. In between times, the word on the grapevine was that flying would be curtailed at the end of the month and RAF Bassingbourn would no longer be an OCU. I was getting decidedly edgy. I had about five weeks to go before my time was up, and I just knew I would fall foul of this arse-hole WO. I reckon this guy had been busy in between times, gleaning information about all the skivers and the bad boys on the camp. When the time was right, he was going to hit us! If you can play devil's advocate, it's a great way to work out what the opposition is thinking! I was not only a skiver, I was a leading bad boy as well. So I had to be near the top of the WO's hit list!

Finally, it was my turn to pay a visit to the bent doctor. In fact, I made doubly sure I was very 'sick' until a few days before my time was up. So I never had the pleasure of any confrontations with the arse-hole WO! It's a funny old world, isn't it, and we humans are a complex lot to say the least. I'd detested national service and spent more time and energy dodging and skiving my way through it than taking the opportunity of learning something useful. But suddenly, and don't in God's name ask me why, I was sad to be leaving!

CHAPTER FIVE

HOMEWARD BOUND

The final goodbyes to my many good mates on the camp made for quite a traumatic and strange finale to my time at RAF Bassingbourn. Even though I'd detested the whole scenario of national service from day one, we had managed to bond together as a band of brothers in the face of authority and adversity. I had been institutionalised for some two years, and now it was time for me to face the real world again. Our mentor Bootsie would be leaving a few weeks after me, and it was he who had organised my going-away piss-up. Bootsie stood up on one of the rickety chairs and, raising his tin mug full of light ale, he said, 'I'd like you to raise your mugs, lads, and drink a toast to my ol' mate Alf.'

He then took a long swig of his drink and wobbled a little on his chair before continuing. 'Despite all the fiddles we've been at from day one, it looks likely we're gonna go 'ome without doing any extra porridge – unless, of course, my randy ol' mate has been rumping one of the officer's wives and put her up the spout.' That brought a round of hysterical laughter from the rest of the boys, followed by ribald remarks like, 'You'd 'ave to be 'ard up to rump one of them old dogs. Most of them look like a bleedin' advert to keep death orf the roads!' That remark nearly brought the house down. The guys were all getting a bit boozy and laughing at the soppiest jokes. Then my right-hand man Half-Pint joined in the fun. 'I've 'eard that our Alf ain't too fussy wot they look like,' he said, with a wicked grin on his face. 'I 'eard,' he went on, 'that our ol' mate rumped Scapa Flo when he woz on jankers a while back.' I waited until the laughter had died down before I went for the lying little bastard. Half-Pint knew I was coming and started jumping onto the beds in an effort to escape, screaming out in mock terror and laughter, 'Help, I'm being molested by the bloke who torpedoed the lovely Scapa Flo, the Belle of RAF Bassingbourn!'

Then I was too pissed to chase him any more and Half-Pint was too pissed to run away any more. So we just lay on the floor side by side while the guys poured beer all over us! I know that's common practice when they launch a new ship. But as for wetting the head of a national service erk on his way out, who knows, it may well have started a new tradition! I looked at Half-Pint lying there and smiled to myself as I remembered all the punch-ups we'd been involved in over the last eighteen months or so. How could a mere slip of a boy like Half-Pint possibly turn into such a vicious animal when the red mist descended on him? Okay, so I had the physique with the big, broad shoulders and the broken nose. But, believe me, I was just a big old pussy-cat when it came down to real street-fighting. As a laid-back sort of guy, I'd weigh up my options before steaming in and maybe getting a good hiding. But not Half-Pint. When he was possessed by the red mist, he would pick up just about anything to use as a weapon, whether it be a bottle, a chair, or even a table! I'd had literally to drag him off his adversaries many times before he beat the shit out of them. He would lie there panting, with me sitting on him, until the red mist started to lift and he could return to the normal world. Then, almost as though he had been suffering a recurring nightmare that he couldn't control, he would say to me, 'Wot's 'appening mate? I fink I've 'ad another one of my funny turns!' Most of the time he couldn't even remember what had happened! Yeah, Half-Pint was a real good mate, but I often wonder if his uncontrollable temper ever led him to the Old Bailey on a murder charge!

We eventually sobered up, and I poodled off to the stores to hand in my paybook and all of my gear. I couldn't help but recall the very first time I had reported to the same office all that time ago, wearing my 'postman's hat', my neatly pressed uniform and my shiny boots. Now all that gear was crammed into my kit-bag, only fit to be dumped, and I looked the business in my sharp whistle and flute and my crocodile 'St Louis Blues' (shoes). All the guys that passed me by were giving me envious and longing glances – they just knew I was homeward bound. As for me, I was loving it and I couldn't wait to get out of the camp.

Finally, it really was time to say my goodbyes to all the lads for the last time. It's very difficult to describe the conflicting emotions that were welling up inside me. For sure, I wanted out. But this had been my home

‘All smile for the camera, lads!’ *(RAF Museum, Hendon)*

for many months and these guys were all my friends, and you can’t just walk away without feeling sentimental and a little tearful can you? We’d shared some bad times, but we’d also had some great times and some good laughs. It was almost like having been thrown into a giant melting-pot. The weaker ones sank to the bottom and maybe blew their effing heads off. But most of us had faced up to the situation and tried to make the best of it. Maybe I’m biased, but I found that the London cockneys, blessed with natural humour, had handled the situation better than most. If they were deep, deep in the shite, unlike some other airmen who would sink into utter despair they would simply make a joke out of it and laugh it off! So I said my last tearful goodbyes, picked up my battered, old suitcase and went out of the door for the final time. The chaps had the last laugh on me, though. As I walked briskly down the path, I heard them whistling ‘Colonel Bogey’ in time to my paces. Some of the chaps were singing the

'Bags of swank, lads! Really swing those arms, now!' *(RAF Museum, Hendon)*

impromptu Army words to the song: 'Boll-ocks, they make a fine good stew, Boll-ocks, and the same to you . . .'. Yeah, I thought to myself, with a lump in my throat. Definitely an experience I will never forget, to my last breath. But, I thought, the RAF won't get me again, no way, even though I had been informed by the adjutant that I was on stand-by for three years and, in the event of hostilities or war, I could be called up again. For sure, they might need clever radar people like Nige the plonker in future conflicts, but who would want me, a Mrs Mopp with no talent? Anyway, war or no war in the future, I had done my bit and they'd have to catch me if they wanted me again! A few short years down the line when the Suez Crisis blew up, I was on my toes and ready to do a runner in the event of a call from the RAF. I make no bones about it – I had already organised a 'safe-house' for myself, and no way would I be going back!

I reached the guardhouse by the exit to the camp for the very last time and was greeted by another old face ambling across, puffing on a ciggie and wearing a big grin. This was one of our old gang, cruelly nicknamed

'Lurch'. He was a lovely bloke, was Lurch. A huge guy, well over 6ft tall and with massive shoulders, a true gentle giant. It would be unkind to call Lurch simple, but in reality he *was* 'a few coppers short upstairs', hence his nickname! But he had a heart of gold and he loved his Mum to bits. 'You orf then, mate?' he enquired, giving me a friendly bear-hug that almost took my breath away. 'You're damn right I'm off, mate,' I replied. 'I can't wait to go down my local and have a pint with all my mates.' He then squeezed my hands so hard that I thought my eyes would water and, looking deep into my eyes, he said in his simple and almost childlike manner, 'You've been a good mate to me, Alf, and I might 'ave gone on the run if it 'adn't been for you. I've told my Mum all about you and she wants you to come round one day for Sunday dinner.' I smiled at the innocence of this huge hulk of a man. He had the massive physique of a heavyweight boxer and could probably knock you spark out with one of his massive fists, but his brain and his reasoning just weren't quite up to scratch. How could I tell my lovely, gentle giant that going from London to Cornwall for Sunday dinner with him and his Mum was not on? So, I did what I do best: I waffled my way past the problem. 'Yeah, that'll be great, mate, I'd look forward to that,' I said, clasping his huge hand in a final goodbye. 'I've got your address and you've got mine, so we'll make a meet when you've done your time, okay?'

Then I strode out of the camp for the very last time, only turning round to give a wave to the massive figure of Lurch. I never saw Lurch again – mind you, we were an unlikely duo in the first place. Me, Jack the Lad from 'the Smoke' with plenty of chat and plenty of front. And Lurch, this massive and innocent country boy who had stood the butt of our cruel jokes for nearly two years. In fact, I was the only person who knew his Christian name, and I'd sworn him to secrecy early on in our friendship for his own benefit. Unfortunately for a guy who grew up a bit simple, his parents had named him Simon! I shudder to think of all the stick he would have had to endure if that had become common knowledge in the camp. Anyway, he was happy with his nickname Lurch, even if he didn't really understand the connotations attached to it!

I sat having a quiet ciggie at the bus stop, right next to the wire fence that bordered RAF Bassingbourn. I smiled to myself as I remembered going over that fence so many times and hitching so many lifts. How I never got caught, thrown in the glasshouse and made to do another extra six months of my national service, I'll never know! Especially as I'm positive that my flight looie knew exactly what I was up to every weekend, because he often made remarks to that effect. One of my mates at the time even recalls a tale about me purloining an ambulance late at night, absolutely 'rat-arsed' after my boozy demob party. Legend has it that I drove it up the runway, thereby preventing flying, and as punishment was made to fly in the Canberra display team taking part in an aerobatics display at Farnborough. While I can't refute the first allegation because I can't remember a thing about my demob party, I know I never went up in a Canberra and performed aerobatics – I would rather have deserted with my 'yellow flag'!

I stubbed out my ciggie as the bus came up, took a big lungful of air and never looked back on where I had found real friendship, but sadly wasted nearly two years of my life!

Home Again

The final train journey to King's Cross was uneventful, as was the ride on the trolley bus up Caledonian Road. I got off the bus at Copenhagen Street, walked up the road about 50yd, then turned left at the petrol station into Twyford Street, with the old Caledonian Road Baths on the other corner. I looked at the huge, red-brick wall of the old Cally Baths as I walked past and smiled to myself at my memories. The many times at night our gang had thrown up our rope and our grappling iron and pulled ourselves up that same wall. We never had any dough to buy a ticket for the fights, but we never missed a show! The original goal-posts I had chalked on the wall all those years ago were still there. A later generation of kids had re-chalked them, but my old site was still being used by potential soccer stars of the future. I fondly remembered the many hours I had spent, all on my own, kicking a ball at those goal-posts. I'd start by whacking the ball against the wall, then volley it back with both feet, at whatever angle it came at me. Then I would head my volleys back against the wall and control it expertly as it came back. In retrospect, those endless hours of whacking a ball against that wall gave me good control on the football field further down the line in my career.

The quaint little terraced houses on Twyford Street still looked as they had since the Victorian era. Yet it was a strange experience when I returned to my old stamping grounds recently to do some research on this book. In fact, I hardly recognised my old street. Whether by design or purely by accident, the Council developers of the 1960s had managed to create two totally different communities, one either side of the main road. The whole area on 'my' side of the road, all the way north from the Canal Bridge right through to opposite the dreaded Pentonville Prison, a distance of half a mile or so, had been razed to the ground. Those quaint old terraced houses had been replaced by an assortment of Council blocks and maisonettes, now looking decidedly the worse for wear after just forty years. I reckon the old terraced houses would have lasted the course a lot better! Strangely, the other side of Caledonian Road, with more or less the same houses, albeit some larger ones, had hardly been touched by the planners. Consequently, these old houses are now worth an absolute fortune and are much sought after by the middle classes, who have completely gentrified the area. So in one fell swoop the local Council had succeeded in creating two completely different communities, divided only by Caledonian Road. One side seemed to be for the Council 'have-nots', who couldn't possibly afford those house prices, and the other side solely for the professional 'outsiders', many of whom continued to shop not locally, for the benefit of the local community, but at the posh stores like Harrods and Fortnums! I remember early in my journalistic career I was asked to do an article by the *Sunday Times* about the 'gentrification' of my 'manor', together with a photo of my good self. The number of angry letters the paper received from the irate outsiders was considerable. It appeared that I had struck a raw nerve with my truthful, if sarcastic, comments!

My old Mum answered the street door and welcomed me home. It wasn't exactly the home-coming reserved for returning heroes, not that I placed myself in that category! But my old Mum could never have been described as overemotional, or excitable. I recall a few years back when me and my mates were mad keen on our cycling and youth hostels and sometimes we used to go touring all over the West Country for two or three weeks. I often remember coming home absolutely skint and starving hungry. My Mum would come to the street door, just as she was doing now, and casually say, 'Did you 'ave a nice time, Alfie?' All I got this time around after 'valiantly' serving Queen and Country for two years was, 'Don't bang the door, Alfie, 'cos your Dad is 'aving a rest.'

I followed Mum down the dark passageway to the kitchen, remembering to step over the holes in the floorboards on the way. And when I say 'holes', I mean holes. If one of your feet went through one of these you could finish up with a hernia! Believe it or not, even as late as the early 1950s our dingy kitchen was still lit by gaslight, with gas-mantles! For all my readers out there who aren't familiar with gas-mantles, let me enlighten you. Their fragility reminded me very much of butterfly wings. When a hole appeared in their fragile make-up you needed to carefully unscrew the old one ready for replacement. However, just the slightest touch of a finger on the new gas-mantle and it would disintegrate into dust. Just a 'glimmer' into Victorian London! I wandered out into the old scullery and chuckled to myself when I saw the tin bath – that object certainly evoked old memories of sharing the water with my sisters and brother! Then out into the tatty little garden and a quick peep into the always freezing cold outside loo. How many times did we kids have to sit around cutting the daily paper into squares? And then pierce a hole in the squares and thread some string through to make a homemade toilet roll? There was no such thing as 'soft tissue' in those far-off days!

My mind wandered back to when we had first moved into the place. After returning from evacuation, our family had shared our Nan's house for quite some time. My old Mum was a real grafter and was always out at the crack of dawn doing her charring. She got friendly with this old lady after she did some cleaning for her, and the old lady offered her the downstairs of her house in Twyford Street, and that's how we moved in. Us kids thought the old lady was a bit of a witch. Whenever we saw her she was wearing the same grubby Victorian-style dress, with a high, stiff collar and square shoulder pads, and tatty shawl wrapped around her. An old-fashioned pair of black bootees could be seen poking out from under her long dress. Her hat was always the same – a grubby pink number, with a pink silk ribbon hanging down her neck. You couldn't help but notice the huge silver hatpin that pierced the bunched-up silver hair. It looked for all the world as though it went right through her head and out the other side!

My old Dad was convinced that the old lady had bundles of dough, and when she suddenly died he was up in her flat desperately searching for the dosh – even before the doctor had arrived. He never did find any dough, and for the rest of his life he convinced himself that she had sewn the money into her Victorian outfit. He told anyone who would listen that the undertakers must have got the dough! Eventually, he was offered the house for £400. Okay, so that sounds a pittance by modern standards, but £400 in postwar London to a family man who was always in the pubs and forever out of work would be like forty grand today. My old Dad took his theory of the missing dough to his grave. He was totally obsessed with what he believed had happened to the old lady's money, and whenever things were bad – which was often, thanks mainly to his boozing – he would start prattling on, if only he had found that money in her bloody flat. The simple fact that any monies he might have found wouldn't have even belonged to him, and so his keeping the dough would have been perceived as stealing, just never entered his head. Sadly, my old Dad was one of life's losers, always going on about 'when my ship comes home' or 'when I win the pools'. He needed to have a pipe-dream to keep him going in his make-believe world!

Over the next few days, I had time and space to sit and ponder my options for the future. And these were looking a bit thin on the ground! My football career seemed to be heading nowhere because Leyton Orient hadn't asked for my return on my loan from the Southern League club. I had been approached by a Southampton scout after he had seen me playing for RAF Bassingbourn, but I had turned down the invitation of a trial. Who wants to live in crappy digs in Southampton after being two years away from home? Okay, so I could still earn a few quid every Saturday, but it wasn't quite the career I had envisaged. Finally and far too late, like most teenagers, I was regretting the lost opportunity of not having learned a trade during my two years in the RAF. Life is a strange phenomenon, isn't it? If only we could have the wisdom of maturity in our early years, it would certainly make things a lot easier later in life. I could have easily picked up a good trade in the RAF and been paid while I was being taught. But no, not me. If I had put half as much effort into learning as I had into skiving, then I would have had a skilled job to take up now. But, I thought, there's no good crying over spilt milk. I had made my bed – now I had to lie in it!

My job options were limited as an unskilled person. The biggest earner by far was 'the Print', but you needed big bucks or a close relative already in the trade to buy your union ticket into this lucrative world. In those far-off days, the unions were all-powerful and basically dictated the staffing levels. Consequently, every single one of the national newspapers was grossly over-staffed, with crazy and ludicrous demarcation lines for working practices. I recall a good mate of mine got himself a job in the Print, thanks to the help of his Dad, who I remember was 'Father of the Chapel'. At the time, and not being familiar with union jargon, I honestly thought his Dad was a vicar in a church! My mate was on nights and he was instructed by the union guy to sweep up all the white paper on the machine-room floor. Cross my heart, it's the God's honest truth – my mate nearly caused a strike all over Fleet Street by inadvertently sweeping up the brown paper as well! It's hard to take in, but dealing with the brown paper was some other guy's job! These ludicrous working practices, crazy and ridiculous demarcation lines and almost total anarchy from the top-heavy staff were all doomed to come to a sticky end in the very near future.

What follows is a classic example of top-heavy staffing on the national newspapers. Whenever we all went out boozing on a Saturday night, eventually moving on to late houses in the Clerkenwell area, we would always encounter a pub full of guys in the Print. Let me pause a moment and explain the strange licensing hours of late houses. In those far-off days, all the pubs around our manor in Islington closed at 10.30 p.m. But if you crossed the boundary at the Angel and went down City Road into Clerkenwell, you could drink until well after 11.30 p.m. So we'd all pile into a cab and stroll into the Nelson Pub to continue our drinking with the guys from the Print. Now, these guys were supposed to be employed by the Sunday papers on a Saturday night as casuals for 'stringing'. That entailed stringing the bundles of papers as they came off the huge printing machines. But because of the gross overstaffing, they'd clock-in at the start of their shift and then take it in turns to spend the night in the pub! The bottom really fell out of the fiddle when the Inland Revenue couldn't help but notice some of the weird signatures on the bulky wage packets. How could the taxman possibly get his dough from 'Mickey Mouse', 'Donald Duck' or even 'Frank Sinatra'? In effect it became so blatant it had to come a tumble!

A decade or so down the line, the Australian millionaire Rupert Murdoch who owned the *Sun*, the biggest-selling tabloid of its day, took his revenge. He hated the print unions, especially after they had refused to print a sensational front-page picture of Arthur Scargill, the militant miners' leader, giving what the unions said could be wrongly interpreted as a Fascist salute during one of their violent strikes. The cunning Murdoch knew full well that Maggie Thatcher was hell-bent on destroying the militant miners. After that he calculated that she would target the next group of militant unionists, the printers. He laid his plans well. Nobody, but nobody, suspected that the new factory being erected in Wapping was anything whatsoever to do with the newspaper magnate Murdoch. Then whispers started coming out about this high-tech establishment with dozens of modern computer consuls inside. The print unions saw the danger much too late. Murdoch swiftly moved his entire operation from Fleet Street to Wapping and every single one of his journalists, most of them members of the NUJ, was given a brutal alternative: come to Wapping or lose your jobs. Only a handful of them stayed true to their union beliefs! But in all fairness to them, they did have families to support.

So Murdoch, with shrewd planning, had pulled it off against all the odds. He got 'Fortress Wapping' up and running without a single printer on site. The violent scenes on the Wapping picket lines are well documented and lasted for a whole year. But the ultimate nail in the printers' coffin came early on in the picket. They had wrongly assumed that Murdoch wouldn't be able to distribute his papers because the Trucker's Union were supporting the picket and no way would they carry his papers. But Murdoch had done his homework well by buying a haulage company called TNT and manning it with non-union drivers. The print unions finally realised the inevitable when these huge TNT lorries rolled out of Fortress Wapping to loud screams of 'SCABS!' So, the militant dockers had bit the dust, as had the miners, and now the all-powerful print unions had been broken. Who was next on Maggie's hit list?

But I digress. The Print was a no-no for me. That left doing some portering in one of the markets. Again, another closed shop, controlled totally by the unions. Smithfield Meat Market was a classic example of union domination. You could see more bashed-in noses and cauliflower ears down there than anywhere else in London! If you were an ex-professional boxer – preferably a former champion – you'd sail through the union test! The chances of getting a job in the old Billingsgate Fish Market were even more remote. I can well remember the old pugs with their battered faces, some of them former household names, sitting patiently at the bottom of Fish Street Hill, swigging their booze and just waiting to help one of the porters 'up the hill' for a couple of bob. In those days the well-known pro boxers were always surrounded by a hoard of hangers-on, who quickly had it away on their toes when their hero got a good hiding in the ring and lost his title. But the former champs had got the taste of the high life, plus a taste for the hard stuff. So, these once super-fit guys were now reduced to drinking 'meths' and helping to push a barrowful of stinking fish up the hill, just for money to fuel their alcohol addiction.

It was the same story down Spitalfields, The Borough and Covent Garden Market. Union domination, or nepotism, was the name of the game. Suddenly, and for reasons I still don't really understand to this very day, my three uncles, all long-serving porters down Covent Garden, didn't want to know me in any job search. Maybe it was because they had already eased their own sons into the market and had used up their quota of union favours. Or, quite possibly, I had got myself a bad reputation first time around!

WORKING ON 'THE RAIL'

For us North London boys that just left working on 'the Post', up at the Mount Pleasant Sorting Office or on 'the Rail', down at the King's Cross Depot in York Way. Now, back in the 1950s, the attraction of any of these jobs wasn't the gross weekly wage. To be perfectly blunt, our first questions to the guys we knew were presently working there were, 'Is there plenty of overtime?', or, 'Are there any fiddles, or chances for a bit of thieving?' I didn't fancy 'the Post', simply because you'd go down for a very long stretch if you were caught thieving from the Queen's Mail! So I eventually took a job on 'the Rail'. In those days, as with the dockers, every single package was handled by the loaders, either trollied off or onto the goods wagons shunted into the depot every day. I was quite amazed at the thieving culture that pervaded the whole depot. Everyone was at it in some way or other. My fellow loaders would whisper info to me as I passed with my trolley. 'If you want sweeties or chocs, mate, there's been a "breakage" in the Newark wagon.' No, I thought to myself, I'm not getting involved for the sake of some sweets. Then another loader would whisper as I went by, 'If you wanna make it with your bird, check out the nylons in the Notts wagon.' And so it went on. The old 'tea-leaves' knew the exact contents of every single package they were handling, and God only knows how much 'hooky-gear' went out on the lorries! I needed to get out of this den of iniquity a bit lively otherwise I'd finish up getting nicked. So I applied for driver training and eventually gained my licence to drive any lorry for British Rail, or anyone else for that matter. I made a bit of a cock-up when applying for a job as a driver, assuming quite wrongly that I was applying for a position at the King's Cross Depot. For sure I got the job but, unknown to me, this depot was miles from where I lived.

Now I was a fully fledged Scammell or lorry driver and proud of it. For the benefit of my younger readers, the old Scammell Scarab was an articulated lorry and the unit, believe it or not, had a single front wheel. It had been ordered specifically by British Rail to take over from the thousands of horses and carts they were presently using for deliveries. They stipulated that the new vehicle should have a very tight turning circle compared to the horses and carts, hence the single front wheel. No synchromesh gearboxes or posh automatics on these old dogs – you needed to double-declutch with feeling and crash the gears through. And not even a starter motor. Just switch on the ignition, and make doubly sure you were in neutral. Then press down on the accelerator and the old girl jumped into life. I believe the top speed was a pedestrian 20 miles an hour! But the Scammell was a loveable old girl, and you could really throw her around when reversing into the loading bay. Then, put the brake on the trailer and jump back into the unit. Pull up a handle, put the old girl into forward drive and, hey presto, the unit and the trailer were parted! The old Scammell Scarabs became very popular with many other major haulage companies and were responsible for the eventual demise of most horses and carts. I believe the quaint old Scammells lasted for over a decade before being replaced by more modern vehicles.

My new depot delivered many loads down the old Royal Docks, and I deliberately refrain from naming it because a few years down the line I was arrested and charged with major criminal offences. But my pitiful efforts at thieving looked like child's play compared to some of the strokes pulled by the experienced dockers. What you have to realise is that way back in the 1950s every single item of cargo was handled by the stevedores and dockers. The stevedores loaded and unloaded the ships and the dockers took the cargo to and from the ships on the quayside. So, if the dockers required a nip of whisky or rum, or some fags, or just about anything else, there would be an 'accident' on the quayside and the 'breakage' would be duly reported to the supervisor. He would instruct one of the gang to trolley the accident to his office. For sure, some bottles of booze would be smashed and cartons of ciggies crushed, while many more would mysteriously disappear. Obviously fallen into the water, would be the official explanation – but only after the office staff had allegedly taken their whack of the goodies as well! Go to any boozer or any café outside the dock gates at any time and you could buy anything 'hooky' you required, all at half price to the right face!

However, the total union domination of the docks made it very scary for an ordinary guy like me. It was the nearest thing to George Orwell's *Big Brother* that I have ever experienced. The dockers did what they wanted, when they wanted. I recall one day when I was still a bit green in the ways of the docks. I had one very small parcel to get rid of down the Victoria Docks, and that was my load finished for the day. I lifted it off my lorry, picked up my delivery sheets and headed past a huge queue of lorries waiting to be unloaded. I strolled up to the loading bay and noticed a group of dockers sitting around, drinking tea and smoking fags. I tossed the parcel onto the loading bay and shouted out in a matey fashion, 'If you've got a minute, guv, could somebody sign this for me?' Well, for one minute I thought I'd called them a bunch of poufs because they all stood up and approached me with menacing looks on their weatherbeaten faces. The little old geezer, he must have been the foreman of the gang, said in a squeaky cockney voice, 'If you don't pick up your bleedin' parcel and go back to your motor a bit sharpish and queue up like everyone else, I'll call in the union convener and he'll shut down the docks.' So I had to spend the rest of the day queuing up with one soppy little parcel, while huge lorries with massive loads were unloaded in front of me. Isn't it any wonder that British Rail was losing so much dough before the arrival of Dr Beeching?

The militant dockers were always calling lightning strikes over some minor issue or other. In effect they could, and did, hold the shipowners and the government to ransom. This was particularly evident down at the Tooley Street wharves, because these took all the perishables like Danish bacon, butter and so on. How strange that some fifty years after the dockers' demise, the new City Hall of Mayor 'Red Ken' Livingstone graces the Tooley Street area! The nail in the dockers' coffin, and the final straw that broke any remaining public support, came when the dockers refused to unload a shipment of Danish bacon at Tooley Street. The unions argued with the shipowners, who were panicking like mad in case their precious cargo went mouldy, and finally a compromise was agreed to solve the predicament. But what a weird compromise, I thought at the time. The dockers would go back and unload the cargo only on condition that the shipowners paid them all the overtime they would have earned if – and this is the killer punch – they hadn't gone on strike in the first instance!

The Port of London Authority and the shipowners had had enough of the union blackmail and the bad press they were receiving. And like Rupert Murdoch, a decade or so later, they made up their minds to destroy the unions once and for all! First question: how to prevent their ships having to unload in the all-powerful union heartland of the Royal Docks? And question two: how to stop all the pilfering and major thieving that was costing them fortunes in insurance? Answer to both: build a new port at the mouth of the Thames at Tilbury and make it a container port, and ensure that the containers would be sealed! So, these sealed containers would be hoisted off and onto the ships, directly from and onto waiting lorries, and no dockers would be required! The dockers' unions tried their damnedest to stop this container port being built because they knew full well it would signal the end of their reign. But everyone had had enough, and the public were sick to death of the constant petty stoppages.

After many years of hectic legal wranglings, the container port at Tilbury was finally up and running. All parties excluding the unions were onto a winner. The shipowners didn't have to pay charges to the pilots of the Port of London Authority for taking them up and down the river, and they now had thousands of acres of prime real estate to sell. The final end of the militant London dockers and their elected leader, a certain influential rabble-rouser called Jack Dash, came swiftly and without any sympathy. Almost overnight, thousands of dockers were put out of work and many thousands of East End families suffered as a consequence. For sure, they got a golden handshake, but their jobs represented a golden lifestyle and that had now gone forever. Now, don't get me wrong. As a working-class guy, I'm all for unions and union representation. But when the tail starts wagging the dog, that creates a problem. And when the unions attempt to take on the establishment, that's a definite no-contest. Nobody, but nobody, ever takes on the establishment and wins.

Now, some four decades down the line, the area of the old Royal Docks has been successfully converted and rebuilt to accommodate thousands of new homes, the huge office complex of Canary Wharf, plus a profit-making venue for European flyers, the City Airport. I still feel pangs of sentimentality whenever I get a fare in my cab down to the City Airport. All the old pubs and cafés are still there, but whereas in the old days they would be bursting at the seams with stevedores, dockers and lorry drivers, now they are just a shadow of their former glory. One of my favourite sayings is, 'Nothing is forever'. The cataclysmic and sudden demise of the all-powerful dockers and their dominant unions makes this saying even more prophetic. Even with the benefit of hindsight, I honestly don't think they could have survived for much longer – Maggie Thatcher or not! As with the miners, the printers and any other unions who believed they could muscle the establishment, their cards were well and truly marked by the people who held the real power.

As for me, well, my earlier visits to Borstal and even my RAF national service hadn't taught me to keep on the straight and narrow. However, the new focus in my life was my wife. I had met a very attractive girl at Christmas time 1955, and despite the fact that Nicolette was convent-educated at Brompton Oratory School and spoke very posh, she agreed to be my wife and we were married a couple of years later – we will celebrate our golden wedding anniversary in 2007! I wanted the good things in life for Nicolette and, sad to say, I was prepared to do just about anything to get them. In my defence, I had unknowingly moved from one den of iniquity to a place where you could count all the honest guys on the fingers of one hand! For starters, the 1950s was a decade of decadence; everyone was at the 'hey-diddle-diddle'. Certainly in my manor it was a recognised culture of thieving by the have-nots. All of us guys in our early twenties had suffered hunger and abuse in the war as evacuees. We had returned to our homes, if they hadn't been destroyed by German bombs or 'Doodlebugs', in postwar London and been denied adequate food or even enough coal for our Mum's fire. We had to start thieving to buy black-market gear off the spivs, who themselves were flogging stolen gear! It was not unlike the terrible drugs spiral of today, where the addicts have to steal just for a fix. I know that times were hard for all the working classes and not everyone took to thieving. However, I had the opportunity to make some quick money, and I took it even though it was never what I would term as 'comfortable money'. Every single knock on our door was enough to make me want to wet myself!

In all honesty, the security at the railway depots in those days was almost non-existent, and everyone was at it. Again, before the advent of sealed containers, every carton or parcel was handled by the workforce and the top thieves knew the contents of every single package just by reading the maker's name. One such name that sticks out in my mind is St Michael, the brand name of Marks & Spencer. The top tea-leaves would give us young drivers a pull and say they had a 'dozen St Michael's' to move off the loading bay and we'd be in for a 'pony', twenty-five pounds! What they were saying, in effect, was that they'd nicked twelve cartons of Marks & Spencer's gear from one of the wagons and stashed it on the loading bay. If we consented to load it onto our lorries we'd make twenty-five quid after the transfer outside. Now, a pony represented something like two or three weeks' wages back in those days. And in all honesty, the young drivers found it was a piece of cake. Everyone joined in the thieving merry-go-round! After all, it was common practice to give the guy on the weighbridge a 'drink' on your way out, so that he put a bit of extra tonnage on your daily load. And you gave his mate a 'drink' when you were weighing in your load at the completion of your daily round for a bit more extra tonnage. It didn't end there in this culture of fiddling. You needed to give the duty foreman a 'drink' because he had clocked you in one hour before you had arrived in the morning. And his mate was clocking you out with an extra hour's overtime after you left for home.

The whole system on the Rail in those days was permeated from top to bottom with fiddles. Even the senior foreman with the gold braid on his hat had a piece of the action – so I was told by the top cop after my arrest. He took a cut of the 'drinks' from every one of his fellow foremen! You needed to look long and hard and from top to bottom at my depot to find any guy who was straight at that time. So if it was perceived by the workforce that the culture of fiddling was seeping down from the top, then everyone wanted some of the easy money, not least of all little ol' me! So, I was also tempted onto the 'gravy-train'. I'm certainly not about to make inane excuses in defence of my illegal involvement, but I often ask myself the pertinent question, what's the difference between straightforward thieving and accepting bribes to falsify overtime and tonnages on lorries on a regular daily basis? In purely legal terms, one is called 'robbery' and the other is called 'fraud'. But the police had their own perception of the scenario. It's the 'peasants' who are doing the thieving, they deduced, while it's the middle management who are committing the fraud. So, if we lock up all the peasants, no problem. But we need middle management to, well, middle manage British Rail!

Being on the thieving spiral is a bit like playing the one-armed bandit in a casino. If you get a result early on, then you carry on playing until you lose, or get caught! By this time I had been affiliated as a 'carrier' to one of the most notorious groups at my depot. Now, here's the rub. Once you'd taken the pledge to join the firm, as with many other criminal conspiracies, you could never get out even if you wanted to. For sure I was getting plenty of dough, but I was only looking for a one-off little 'tickle' at the start – then out! Now I was well and truly involved with the heavies. These guys didn't take any prisoners. If you didn't do what they told you to, you'd either finish up having the shit beaten out of you or they would grass you up to the ol' bill. The final scenario was inevitable. One day much further down the line, I popped home to see my wife before going back to the depot with my load. She was crying her eyes out because the ol' bill had turned my place over and taken away various items they thought may have been stolen. I had no problem there; that was their job. But I took umbrage when my wife told me that the top cop had said he would look after our little baby while I was away doing time. That remark made me really angry, and I vowed to do everything in my power to beat any charge.

My popping home before going back to the depot proved to be my way out, as it enabled me to make a phone call to a certain person who bought loads of hooky gear. This guy could prove conclusively that he bought the stuff in markets all over the UK. So, maybe a possible dead-end for the ol' bill? I tried very hard to look surprised when I returned to my depot and the foreman said, oh-so-casually and with half a sneer, 'When you've cleared your load, the Railway Police would like to have a word with you.' I eventually got round to knocking on the ol' bill's door and was ushered in to see the 'boss-man'. Again, I had to feign a modicum of surprise when he told me that they had turned my flat over earlier in the day. 'It's not looking too good for you, son,' he said, in a fatherly manner. 'We've found a lot of gear in your gaff and we think it's been nicked.' I had decided from the start not to be flash and to stick to my story, whatever the consequences. 'I'm sorry, officer,' I said in my politest voice, 'but I can account for all those purchases.' I then proceeded to give him the name of the market trader I had contacted earlier in the day. This guy had agreed to give evidence on my behalf. In fact, he had been given an offer he couldn't refuse! Either accept the nice few quid my firm were offering him for his services, or get his legs broken! It may sound rather harsh in the light of day, but this guy had made bundles from our long-going operation! Now it was payback time, and his turn to help us.

The rest of the story is predictable. I was duly charged, put on remand, and suspended from my job pending the outcome of my case. During that worrying time of something like nine months, I had two choices: either pick up my cards from the depot and try to find another job, or take a chance that I would beat the rap and stay suspended. If, and it was a very big 'if', I did win my case, then I could claim every single penny I had lost over that past nine months. Being a bit of a gambler, I decided to give the second option a try! I spent the next nine months driving a lorry all over the country. This lorry had been designed as a mobile bedroom to show off the company's expensive mattresses and their top salesman travelled with me. Month after month they asked for my employment cards, and for months I continued to give them dodgy excuses as to why I couldn't present them.

My trial was really scary. I was led into a holding cell and saw a couple of other guys in deep conversation in the corner. Their faces looked very familiar, and that's when I nearly wet myself. This young and very nervous petty thief was actually sharing a cell with the notorious Kray twins! Even as early as the late 1950s the Kray twins had attained a formidable reputation among us London tearaways. They had more or less taken over London's criminal underworld from the old villains like Billy Hill, Jack Spot, Albert Dimes and the Maltese gangs who ran the brothels. Now London had both the Kray firm and the Richardsons, with their notorious enforcers 'Big' Freddie Foreman and 'Mad' Frankie Fraser, all vying for the place of top dog. The twins' following swelled, and the Kray myth and the hero-worship began after they successfully 'defeated' the might of the British Army with their total disobedience of national service rules and regulations.

Despite spending most of their service in the glasshouse, the twins still refused to bow to Army discipline. The Army finally gave it up as a bad job. They got rid of them by giving them a 'DD', a Dishonourable Discharge. But unless you knew the Kray twins, they didn't look at all like your stereotypical villain. Even in the holding cell they were wearing expensive, matching grey suits with the square-cut box jackets that exaggerated their barrel chests. Smart silk shirts, matching ties and expensive-looking black leather shoes completed their attire. I can always remember their hair, thick and black and brushed back without a parting. Their prominent black eyebrows seemed to make their eyes even colder and more intimidating. I nodded to them in a friendly manner when they turned around and stared at me with those cold eyes. Luckily for me we had a mutual friend and after I had shown my respect for them with the accepted friendly greeting of, 'You alright, Ron, you alright, Reg?', I added: 'I'm a mate of Big Patsy out of the Angel.' I then received a long, hard stare from those cold eyes, just checking to see if I was maybe a police plant. Finally, the twins grunted as if satisfied and moved into the corner to discuss something private! I heard later that they had been charged with slashing a guy with a bayonet. But – surprise, surprise – nobody turned up for the prosecution, so there was no case!

When my name was eventually called I left the dimness of the holding cells and the Kray twins, accompanied by an old copper. I climbed the steps to the dock, suddenly entering a scary new world of bright, glaring lights. It seemed as though everyone in the courtroom was staring at me – barristers and solicitors and a stern-looking judge in his wig. Believe me, friends, standing up in the dock all on your lonesome is the most frightening thing that I have ever experienced. Just remember, if you want to be a villain this is what you have to endure regularly! Suffice to say, our man did his bit in the witness box and the judge threw the case out even though they had me bang to rights. I felt quite sorry for the old boy they put into the witness box for the prosecution. This was an honest old guy, dragged up to London from his country village and made to stand up in front of so many people. He looked even more nervous than me – and he was only a witness! My legal team tied him into knots and made him almost call white, black! The boss cop was not a happy bunny!

As for me, I copped for nine months' back wages, plus all the lost overtime, and decided to quit while I was ahead. The word on the grapevine was that I was top of the list for a 'fit-up' from the ol' bill. So, discretion being the better part of valour, I asked for my cards and departed! I read in the press some time later that some person or persons unknown had raided the bonded section of the depot; that is, the section that houses all the big goodies like brandy, whisky and ciggies. Unfortunately the place was burnt to the ground and, sadly, I believe some innocent people died in the terrible blaze. As for me, the future wasn't looking too rosy: mainly down to my laid-back approach to life, I was now an unsuccessful RAF aircraftman, an unsuccessful professional footballer and, lately, an unsuccessful lorry driver for British Rail. My options looked slightly iffy, to say the least. I needed to get my act together in an effort to provide for my wife and baby daughter. Surely I couldn't be washed up at the tender age of twenty-six?

On 'The Knowledge'

Many of my mates were London cabbies by now, and in 1961 they persuaded me to sign on for the dreaded 'Knowledge' of London, something that everyone wishing to become a London cabbie has to endure. But I had a problem: at that time I was still on remand for the serious criminal offence. When the boss-man at the Public Carriage Office – in those days that was the department that controlled London taxis, whereas nowadays it's TfL, Transport for London – anyway, when he saw my 'rap-sheet', or, shall we say, my list of past criminal misdemeanours, he went a bright shade of puce! 'Now look here now, laddie,' he said in a broad Scottish accent, 'we canna be having laddies like you signing on to be a licensed cabbie, when you're no clear of the p'lice the noo.' I took a deep breath and studied this guy to see where he was coming from. Definitely an ex-Army regular, I reckoned. He had a smartly clipped moustache, just beginning to turn grey, and a ramrod-straight back that never seemed to move – even as he walked around the room. He's gotta be an ex-sergeant major in one of the Highland regiments, I thought to myself. In today's world, this guy would have made a dead ringer for 'Mr MacKay', the bolshie senior prison warden in the popular television series *Porridge*. Can't you just visualise the 'Mr MacKay walk'? A ramrod-straight back and a neck that stuck out like a chicken's, looking for all the world like he was going to peck 'Fletcher'!

He spoke again. 'You'll need to come back the noo to register if you're found no' guilty. But, if ye go down, don't bother ever to come back again laddie, is that clear?' Yeah, that was crystal clear. But I had the last laugh as it turned out, by beating the charge and walking free. So, I did return the 'noo'! The 'Knowledge' basically entails riding around the streets of

London on a scooter, sometimes for as long as four years, for no wages, and trying desperately to memorise every street, theatre, restaurant, hospital, town hall, police and train station, in addition to posh gentlemen's clubs, tourist spots, knocking shops and just about everything else of note or not of note, within a 6-mile radius of Charing Cross! You had to face a miserable-looking examiner every fifty-six days and attempt to answer what you thought you had learned, but probably hadn't! My mates informed me that if I stuck at it religiously for a couple of years, then I could be my own boss, with my own taxi, and earn a decent living for my wife and kids.

Nevertheless, I still needed to earn a crust while I was doing the Knowledge. So I decided to train for my PSV (Public Service Vehicle) licence, which enables you to drive a coach. This I managed at the first attempt, and I spent the next year on the Knowledge in the day and driving for George Ewer & Son Ltd, a coach firm based at Stamford Hill, at night. Working nights was actually a 'punishment' for me because I had inadvertently left a mentally retarded young woman at Colchester. Nobody had bothered to inform me about this special pick-up, but the bosses got a right rollicking from the authorities and they made me the fall guy. So I was given what all the other drivers called the crappiest job on the whole coach station: the very last service coach out of King's Cross, the 'Ghost-Train' up to Ipswich and Felixstowe, late every night. I left at 10.30 p.m. and 'swept up' any late passenger at every service stop all the way to Ipswich and Felixstowe. Then it was back to our garage in Ipswich that we shared with the local cabbies for a quick cup of tea and a kip under my blankets on the back seat of the coach. The cabbies used to wake me up at about 5.30 a.m. with a cuppa, ready to pull out at a minute to six. Then I'd return to King's Cross, dump the coach back at Stamford Hill and get on my scooter to do my Knowledge 'runs', followed by a couple of hours' kip in the late afternoon.

Many's the time one of my coach passengers would approach me somewhat nervously in the dark of the night on the open road and ask if I was alright, because I seemed to be talking to myself. We'd have a good laugh together when I explained I was 'calling over' the Knowledge runs and trying to remember them. They would often sit beside me and read out the next sequence of runs from my book, and I would call them over. As luck would have it, this so-called crappiest job on the whole coach station suited me fine and enabled me to have spare time in the day. So, much to the utter amazement of my fellow drivers, I volunteered to do the 'Ghost-Train' full time after I had served my punishment.

My many hilarious experiences while doing the Knowledge and the anecdotes in the daily life of a London cabbie are well documented in my first book, *Cabbie*. And, dare I say it, even my critical cabbie friends reckon it's a great read.

For sure, I had been a rascal for most of my life. But taken into context with the rest of the lads who grew up with me in the postwar era on Caledonian Road, it was about par for the course. Not many people realise that rationing went on in the UK until 1954, so there were never any 'goodies' for us young guys. If you wanted 'extras', it meant the black market and the black market cost a lot of dough. So where did we get that dough from? Thieving!

However, completing the Knowledge after a long, hard slog dramatically changed my complete outlook on life. Having succeeded in gaining my coveted Green Badge and becoming a responsible licensed London taxi driver made for probably my greatest accomplishment in a life of non-achievement, and no way was I going to lose it by getting involved in anything hooky. After a lifetime of being first on the fringe of crime, then later on being heavily involved, I had now, as the born-again Christians like to say, finally seen 'the light'. No way was I prepared to jeopardise all the many months of hard work I had put in to attain my Green Badge. Only the very fittest of young guys could have survived my rigorous lifestyle of working all night and riding around the streets of London all day on a moped for nearly a year! So, no more hooky gear, no shady deals, nor anything just the slightest bit crooked. Mind you, I'll never be quite as straight as your Roman roads!

The rest of my story is positively boring. I trod the straight and narrow and became Mr Nice Guy for the next forty years as a happily married London cabbie, with my lovely wife Nicolette, three wonderful kids and, at the last count, seven grandkiddies! I was fortunate enough to incorporate my passion for writing into my career by becoming a well-known taxi-trade journalist for more than three decades. Then I edited one of the trade publications for almost six years. This enabled me to secure major sponsorships for my next passion, golf. So I organised cabbie golf tournaments for many successful years, taking the finalists over to Spain –

all for nowt! Ask any of the keen cabbie golfers – even after fifteen years or so they still talk about the boozy finals in the sun! Without wishing to blow my own trumpet – would I ever? – my ugly mug has been at the forefront of most things that have happened in the London taxi trade over the past forty-odd years, whether in sport or in politics!

I managed to win the coveted 'Taxi Driver of the Year' award in 1978 – not for my looks, mark you! This event, in aid of the Taxi Drivers' Fund for Underprivileged Children, is a big day in the taxi-trade calendar. The written test is held a month before the final, and the contestants have to answer various multiple choice questions on London; for instance, how many cathedrals are there south of the Thames – one, two or three? The top fifty hopefuls go through to the big final and have a chance to win big bucks.

On finals day the Public Carriage Office examiners, again generously giving up their day of rest for the sake of the charity, lay out an obstacle course. This consists of bollards forming slaloms and imaginary garages, and requires top-notch driving not to knock any of them over and incur penalty points. The final section of the competition takes the entrants out onto the streets of London with a 'stopped clock', which means that no waiting time is registered, just distance. The contestants line up at the exit and are given a sealed envelope containing the names of a dozen landmarks all over London. The year I won the title the list consisted of twelve police stations – quite appropriate for me, you could say! The idea was to arrange these twelve points in a circular fashion, almost as if they were deliveries. A marshal checked you in at each stop and the winner of that section was the driver who had the least amount of money on his meter! I think all the other contestants that year must have taken a bribe, because I won the title by a country mile! My year 'on the throne' was quite exciting, starting with my taxi in the Lord Mayor's Show, following the Lord Mayor's carriage. But you know the old saying that 'after the Lord Mayor's Show comes the shit'? There followed an appearance on *Blankety Blank*, then hosted by Terry Wogan, and yet another Saturday night television quiz, followed by two documentaries on BBC television. Yeah, it was a great year!

As a London cabbie, I love the history and the longevity of our trade, going way back to 1694 when Oliver Cromwell first gave us our Charter. Parliament has renewed it annually for the past 310 years – that's *real* history! The more mature London cabbies such as myself have a deep feeling for the history of our trade and fully comprehend that our purpose-built vehicle is a world 'icon', on a par with the Tower of London, the Houses of Parliament and St Paul's Cathedral. Many tourists to our wonderful city, especially the Yanks, have a ride in the famous London taxi at the very top of their 'wanna-do' lists! Sad to say, some trade organisations are pushing for alternative vehicles for use as London taxis. I have been savaged in the trade press as an 'old dinosaur' simply because I honestly believe that any change from our world-famous vehicle would be a retrograde step. If, in the future, us London cabbies were all driving MPVs, multi-purpose vehicles, then our legendary image would be blurred and the general public wouldn't know, and probably wouldn't care, about the difference between a taxi and licensed private hire. Okay, so our purpose-built taxi *is* expensive and, yes, there is a monopoly. But we must never knock down the bricks we've patiently built for over 300 years. The London taxi trade is renowned for shooting itself in the foot. Surely we won't do it again! If people the world over rightly judge us as the most famous cabbies in the world, then the vast majority of us try to live up to that praise by providing a world-class taxi service.

And now, would you Adam-and-Eve it?, this yobbo from the slums of North London has reached the dizzy heights of a published author. I've been on the telly, I've done about eight radio shows and I've been featured in many papers and magazines. And it doesn't end there. My third book, about the Second World War, the Blitz and my horrendous experiences as an evacuee from war-torn London, should be in the bookshops soon after this second book is published! For sure, the fame is great fun and nobody sniffs at earning royalties. But the very bottom line is the self-satisfaction of dedicating it to my wonderful wife Nicolette.

Thank you kindly for reading my book and I do hope you found it interesting. Remember to try and enjoy every minute of every day, my friends, because life races by so quickly and the future is a mirror you can't look into. As we London cabbies like to say as a fond farewell, I wish you a long life, and be very lucky!

ENDPIECE

While writing this book, I was aware of headlines in the press – and a great deal of television and radio coverage – concerning the families of the four young soldiers who had allegedly committed suicide at Deepcut Army barracks, Surrey. These bereaved families were calling on the government for a public inquiry.

The plot thickened when it was revealed that a former instructor at this barracks had been charged with a string of offences against some young soldiers, including violent bullying, sexual assault and rape. This person was convicted and sentenced to four-and-a-half years in jail. The Surrey police were called in to investigate the four deaths and their report stated that there was no sign of foul play.

There were more revelations in the national press about the 'culture of bullying', not only at Deepcut, but at Catterick barracks as well. A whole list of allegations was published which, if true, would indicate a catalogue of sexual abuses against these young soldiers. But still the government resisted the call for a public inquiry, opting instead for a private inquiry, which is ongoing as I write.

So, you may be asking yourself, what is the link to this story and my stories of RAF national service in the 1950s? The answer is my former camp Bassingbourn, my old stamping ground. Once it had been closed as an OCU and flying had been moved elsewhere, Bassingbourn became an Army camp – but an Army camp with a difference. Many of the young soldiers who were allegedly abused and sexually assaulted had started their Army careers as cadets in pre-Army training at Bassingbourn. When they had finished their course at Bassingbourn, they were posted to either Catterick, Pirbright or Deepcut barracks.

So, rather than wonder where on earth Bassingbourn was situated, as I did all those years ago, you can now pick up on all the latest reports about these terrible allegations and home in on the Hertfordshire and Cambridgeshire borders.

As a father and a grandfather, my sympathy goes out to the families who have lost a daughter or son in such tragic circumstances. They are only campaigning for justice and my heart goes out to them.